EXCEL 2022

The All In One Step-by-Step Guide From Beginner
To Expert. Discover Easy Excel Tips & Tricks
to Master the Essential Functions, Formulas &
Shortcuts to Save Time & Simplify Your Job

Mike Wang

Mike Wang

TABLE OF CONTENTS

Chapter 1

INTRODUCTION TO
MICROSOFT EXCEL

M S Excel is a database program that was created by Microsoft in 1985 for the primary purpose of assisting companies in compiling all of their financial records, as well as annual credit and debit sheets.

Excel is a very powerful application that offers countless opportunities to improve and track the efficiency of our daily tasks. Designed to improve the storing, analysis, and calculations on large sets of data, Excel has the potential to massively boost work productivity and efficiency for the knowledgeable user.

It is disheartening to witness how many people only view excel as a data storage tool, where each data point is manually typed… a brainless task that consumes countless hours of your day.

Excel is much more, it is a very powerful platform with the potential to automate a vast amount of tasks and operations. When used correctly, format templates can be defined and transferred to any future document. Formulas to execute analyses and mathematical operations on large datasets can be typed quickly and adapted to future documents easily. Logic checks can be defined to ensure boundaries or testing conditions are met by your data.

Data can be effectively organized and formatted to build clear, effective, and concise reports that will present your results in a convincing and professional way. The range of tools and functionality available for statistical analysis is immense, allowing users to tackle very large amounts of data.

When you open an Excel sheet, there are 5 main areas that you should be prepared for:

The quick access toolbar: this is a place where all the tools can be accessed from in Excel. A new Excel sheet will only have 3 icons, which are *save, undo* and *redo*. You can always add any other features that you feel are important to this part of the sheet in order to make it easy to access the new features from anywhere.

Excel is very useful for a number of reasons and the most important one here is in order to handle data well. The program offers all the features and the simplicity to enter data and handle it in a much easier way. It has enough grids to be able to manage and handle a large amount of data at a go. Data in Excel can be manipulated with so much ease, thanks to some of the best features like find, copy, paste, highlight, styles, go to, and many more. This makes Excel one of the most important programs in any office. Generation of data is an everyday process in any business and organization and much of this data is important for as long as the business exists.

Excel in Mobile Phones

Microsoft Office software includes all of Microsoft Corporation's core products. When you purchase and install this software on your computer, you gain access to a variety of Microsoft products, including Excel. There are versions of Office available for purchase on the office.com website, as well as in various online and physical retail stores. Microsoft currently sells Office 2019 and Office 365 on their website. They also advertise Microsoft 365, which is more significant (formally Office 365). So, if you don't already have Office installed on your computer, you may upgrade to the 365 edition, which comes with a slew of new capabilities.

Using a Mobile App to Share an Excel File

Follow these steps to share your Excel file once you've finished preparing it:

- Tap the share icon in the top right-hand corner of the Excel interface.
- Choose whether to send your file as an attachment to others via email or to share it through OneDrive.

You may effortlessly collaborate with others when you choose to share using OneDrive. You can transmit it by typing the email addresses of the individuals you want to share it with. You can also obtain a link that you can share with others by emailing it to their phone numbers and sharing it with them through social media platforms such as Facebook and WhatsApp. Keep in mind that OneDrive is a Microsoft cloud storage service.

When you select Share as an attachment, a box will appear where you can enter the email addresses of the people to whom you want to send the Excel file. Simply enter their email addresses, or a single email address if you're only mailing to one person, and then send the file.

Using a Mobile App to Save an Excel Document

I'll also teach you about this important topic. Automatic Excel file saving is enabled by default in the Excel App for smartphones. As a result, you may not need to take any action. If you want to save the file manually and give it a unique name, follow these steps:

- At the top right-hand corner of the workbook interface, tap the ellipsis (three dots arranged vertically).
- Save the file among the options.
- Fill up the blanks with the name you wish the Excel file to have.
- Tap 'Save' to save your file anywhere; you can put it on your phone, which is referred to this device, or you can save it in your OneDrive account.

Where Can I Get an Office Package that Includes Excel?

There are a few places where you may purchase and install Office on your PC. The following are some of the outlets:

The Microsoft and Office websites provide access to the Microsoft Office website.

www.amazon.com is the official website of Amazon.

Walmart is a retailer that can be found at Walmart.

As well as a variety of other physical computer software retailers.

When you go to www.microsoft.com, for example, Microsoft will suggest that you that the Microsoft 365 package for your computer. This is because the software has many useful new features added to the package's components.

When you go to www.amazon.com, on the other hand, you will be taken to the website's home page. Select Software as your search option from the dropdown at the upper left-hand side of the site's search field.

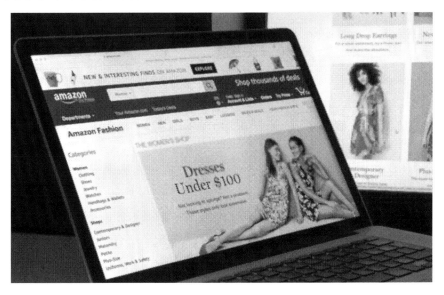

You should utilize the search box on the Indigo Software Company's website, indigosoftware.com, to find the version of Office you wish to install on your computer. The company will walk you through the procedures of installation and activation.

Walmart, like Amazon, still sells various versions of Office software on their website. When you open the site, utilize the search box to look for the Office version you wish to buy. If the version is still available, you can pay for it, download it, install it, and activate it.

You can acquire any Office application you choose from any computer software provider near you. The seller will also walk you through the installation and activation of the application bundle.

Obtaining Free Microsoft Excel

The Microsoft Corporation has just released a new product. It gives you online access to Microsoft Excel without having to pay for the software, but only with limited features. Other Microsoft programs, such as Microsoft Word, Outlook, Publisher, One Note, OneDrive, Skype, and others, are available to you for free. However, because Excel is our main interest, we shall concentrate on it.

You must follow these steps to gain free access to Excel:

Visit the Office website, preferably using your Chrome browser, with your computer connected to the internet.

When you first arrive on the site's homepage, you'll see something similar to this:

If the Sign up for the free version of Office link is not visible on the website's homepage when you visit it, simply click Sign in and then pick Sign up when the link appears. Simply enter your email address under the Create Account section of the new page that appears after you click Sign up. It might be your Gmail, Yahoo, or any other email account.

You'll be logged in to the Office online platform once you've finished setting up your Microsoft account.

You can click Excel once you've logged in. Excel will open after you click it, and you can begin inputting data into the cells. As we progress, I'll teach you more about data entry.

The Importance of the Microsoft Excel Program

The Microsoft Excel application is extremely important in today's culture. Because of its significance, it is the most widely used spreadsheet application in the world today. Excel is extremely vital in our day-to-day operations.

Chapter 2

TERMINOLOGY: WHAT THE BASIC TERMS MEAN

AutoFill: This enables you to copy data to more than one cell easily.

AutoFormat: This is an automatic format application to cells that match predetermined conditions. This could be as simple as size.

Menu: The list of items along the top of the screen; for example, file, insert, page layout, etc.

Name box: Just underneath the Ribbon you have a white box on the left-hand side, it shows the cell reference (default A1) or if you have specified a name for a cell or range of cells, it will show that name.

Spreadsheet: A method of spreading information across a sheet of paper. The screen represents a piece of paper with grid lines.

Worksheet: A page within the Workbook. By default, an Excel Workbook contains 3 worksheets; they are viewed using tabs along the bottom.

Cells: The grid lines make rectangular boxes—known as cells. They are referred to using a letter and a number.

Columns: Cells down a spreadsheet are columns—letters.

Rows: Cells across the spreadsheet are rows—numbers.

Button: A button in Excel is merely an icon that you can click to accomplish a certain operation. Various buttons are utilized to do various tasks. Bold, underline, text aligns, and other buttons are available. A button in Excel can be referred to as a command or a tool.

Workbook: A workbook is a collection of cells that are arranged in rows and columns. When you first open your Excel application, you will interact with that working area. It's the spreadsheet where you type in numbers and text. Many spreadsheets can be contained within a workbook.

Cell: It's the point where a certain row and column meet. Cells can be rectangular or square in shape, depending on the size that an Excel user selects.

Chapter 3

HOW TO USE AND FORMAT
CELLS

Basic Cell Navigation

You can use the cursor keys to move around the cells. Of course, you can just use your mouse to click on the cell that you want to select and edit, but that will be hellish if you are dealing with multiple pages and data.

Fast Page Navigation

Aside from using the cursor keys, you can check out the other cells that you cannot see within your screen or viewport by pressing the Page Up (PgUp) and Page Down (PgDn) keys to move fast upwards or downwards the screen.

Pressing the End button will put Excel into End mode. When Excel is on End mode, pressing a cursor or arrow key will take you to a data region edge, according to the direction of the arrow key that you pressed.

Data Region Edge Navigation

If you want to precisely go to the edge of the data cluster, meaning continuous cells that you have filled up with information, you can use the Ctrl and cursor keys. For example, if you have a 3 x 3 table filled with data, you can go to the bottommost cell in that table by pressing Ctrl and the down arrow button. The same effect will happen if you perform other cursor arrows and Ctrl key combinations.

Remember that these combinations of keys will only work on columns or rows that are filled with continuous data. In case that there is a gap between the tables or cells, an empty cell, the cursor will only go to the edge before the blank cell.

If you are currently editing a cell or have an active cell and you want to quickly move to an adjacent cell, you can use the Enter, Tab, and Shift keys. Note that:

- Pressing Enter will let you move down from the active cell.
- Pressing Shift and Enter will let you move to the cell above.
- Pressing Tab will let you move to the right cell.
- Pressing Shift and Tab will let you move to the left cell.

Another alternative to make it easier for you to send your selection without memorizing all the shortcut keys and combinations is to just press the F8 key. Pressing that will make Excel go into extended selection mode. Once you are in it, just use the navigation keys to extend your selection.

Cell Selection Extension

If you want to select multiple cells in a row or column, you can just hold the Shift button and then use the cursor keys to select the other cells that you want to be included in your selection.

Cell Selection until Data Region Edge

If you want to select all the data within a table or continuous cells in the row or column, you can do that by pressing Shift, Ctrl, and the arrow key that corresponds to the direction of the cells you want to add in your selection resides.

Cell Data Types

Although this may not be known to the occasional Excel user, whenever you type anything into an Excel cell, it is automatically assigned a data type. The data type is used by the application in the background to classify the information it contains and process it more effectively.

The data type of a cell can be viewed and manually changed by the user using the button shown above. When working on large datasets, users should ensure the correct data type is selected for maximum efficiency and effective data processing. Below is a list of the main data types available and their description.

Generic: This is the default data type assigned to a new entry by Excel. It imposes no limit or structure on the cell's content; any combination of alphanumeric characters is allowed.

Number: This data type covers cells that only contain numeric data. Defining the data type helps define a clear structure for a spreadsheet and improve computational speed for Excel's algorithms.

Currency: After assigning this data type to a numeric cell, your local currency symbol will be displayed in the cell. What is particularly useful about this format is that the content of the cell remains a number despite the currency symbol displayed; hence normal operations can be executed on it. This is also useful when typing numbers in as you do not have to retype the currency number every time with a new value.

Short Date: Formatting the data type for dates is very useful because it ensures a standard and constant display format is established. The format for the "short date" format is *DD/ MM/YY*. A standard date format ensures that data processing routines are applicable to all your dates.

Long Date: Same benefits of using a constant date format as described above. The only difference is the display format for this data type "Day Number Month Year." Example: "Wednesday 1 March 2017"

Time: This formatting type will display time in the following structure "hh-mm-ss."

Percentage: This formatting type will convert decimal numbers into percentages. For example, if you type in "0.54" and select the percentage formatting type, "54%" will be displayed in the cell. If you use the cell in numeric calculations, excel will conveniently ignore the % sign and only consider the decimal numeric value.

Fraction: This formatting type will convert decimal numbers into fractions. For example, if you type in "0.6" and select the fraction formatting type, "3/5" will be displayed in the cell. If you use the cell in numeric calculations, excel will conveniently ignore the "/" sign and only consider the decimal numeric value represented.

Scientific: This format is particularly useful when working with large numbers, typically in a scientific or experimental context. If you type in the number "125589" and select the scientific formatting option, the cell will display "1.25 E+5."

Text: This format simply defines the content of a cell as text. It will not change the displayed value or impose any type of formatting. It is rarely used.

Entering Data into the Cell

To enter data into a cell, simply left-click on the cell, this will grant you access to enter your preferred data into the selected cell.

Identifying a Cell Name

As earlier explained, a cell is the intersection between a row and a column. For example, a cell can be named B3, C5, E7, and so on. In the example below, the data was entered into the D-column and row-4.

Quick Summation of Data

Data entered into a cell can be quickly calculated by highlighting the data (left-click the data and drag to the data end) and checking the result (summation) at the bottom right side of the worksheet as shown below.

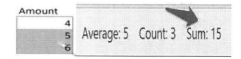

In another way round, you can perform auto sum and let it appear at the cell appearing immediately after the cells containing your data. To do this, simply highlight the data you wish to perform auto sum on and click the auto sum button at the top right side of the worksheet under the home tab.

Naming Cells

Naming this data will make it easier to refer to later, add a name in the Name Box and save it by pressing the ENTER key.

Names cannot contain spaces and must start with a letter, a backslash, or an underscore. Each name must always be unique.

The remaining characters can be underscores, periods, numbers, and letters. Excel will not distinguish capital and lowercase letters. If you wish to make the name, and therefore the cell or group of cells visible to the current workbook as a whole, add the prefix Sheet1! to the start of the name where Sheet1 is the sheet you are basing the data in.

You can also select the group of cells you wish to name, right-click and either choose a name yourself with the Define Name option or let Excel label the data for you with the Pick From Drop Down List option.

Additional naming options can be found on the Formulas tab under the Defined Names Sections.

How to Wrap Texts in a Cell

This feature helps you to prevent longer texts from overlapping into other cells in an Excel spreadsheet. With this, you can display text on many lines instead of one long line.

You can wrap texts in a cell automatically by visiting the Alignment section in the *Home tab.* From the lists, select the Wrap *Text button.*

How to Auto Select Different Cells

You can quickly select rows, columns, cells, and even ranges including the contents of a cell in a worksheet. Here are ways to autoselect cells:

a. Navigate to the last cell within the range you want to select.
b. Press down your shift key.
c. Tap on the cell.
d. With this function, all the cells in the range will be selected.

Resizing Rows and Columns in a Cell

Now, launch Excel and select a document to load. Position the cursor within a cell and tap to highlight it. Go to the ribbon on the right side and press the *Format button.* From the menu, you can click on *Column Row height,* to adjust the height of a Row.

Then, type in the preferred width and click the OK icon.

How to Copy the Contents of a Cell

To copy the contents of a cell, begin by selecting the range of cells. *Press Ctrl + C* on your keyboard or tap on the *Copy button* located in the Home menu. Place your cursor on the cells where you want to paste the contents. You will notice a dashed box around the copied cells.

How to Paste the Contents of a Cell

If you want to move or paste the contents of a cell in an Excel spreadsheet, simply select a range of cells. Press the *Ctrl + X buttons* or click on the Home menu and tap on *Cut.* Locate a cell where you can transfer the data.

Press the *Ctrl + V buttons* or go to the *Home menu* and click on the *Paste icon.* With the copy and paste commands, you can transfer the cells in your worksheet. Locate the cells and *press Ctrl + C* or simply, press the *Copy button.* Then, press *Ctrl + V* or tap on the *Paste button.*

Can you Change the Font and Font-Size of a Cell?

Changing the font and font size of contents within a cell in Microsoft Excel could be done in the following ways:

1. Tap on the *File menu* and select *Options.*
2. Scroll to the dialog box and select the *General bar.*

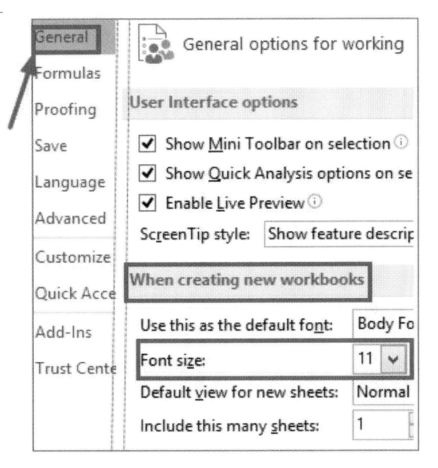

3. Navigate to *When creating new workbooks bar,* a dialog box opens showing the font size. Type in the font size you want.

Underlining Commas in a Cell

If you want to underline commas or other contents in a worksheet, follow these procedures:

1. Select the range of cells or cells to underline all numbers or texts.
2. Double-tap on the cell to underline a segment of it.
3. Then, select the numbers or texts you want to underline.
4. In the Font section on the *Home menu,* tap the Underline.

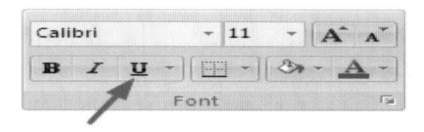

5. If you want to use a double underline, a single accounting underline, or a double accounting underline, tap the dialog box launcher. This is beside the Font. From the underline box, select the type you want to apply.

How to Add Borders to a Cell

If you want to add borders to a group of cells or a cell, select such cells. Go to the *Home menu* and locate the *Font section.* Tap the down arrow beside the *Borders icon.*

A menu pops up with a list of various types of borders. Select the border you want to apply. This will be reflected in the cells.

Deleting a Cell

To delete a cell is simple, first select the cell/row/column as the case may be and navigate to the cell pane at the top-right side of the pane and click delete. This will inquire from you if you are deleting a sheet row or a sheet column or a cell, choose the corresponding option to what you are deleting.

A shorter and faster means of getting this done is by selecting the cell/row/column you wish to delete, then right-click your mouse and select delete.

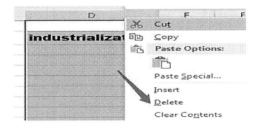

How to Drag and Drop a Cell

Here are the methods of moving cells with drag and drop features:

a. The first step is to locate the range of cells to move and select them.
b. Position your mouse pointer on the edge of the chosen range. This pointer turns to the symbol of a hand or four-sided arrow.
c. Press down the left mouse button and drag the cells to any location you want them to be.

How to Modify the Text Alignment of your Border in Cells

You can align texts in a cell using vertical alignment and horizontal alignment.

Horizontal Alignment

For horizontal alignment, you have left alignment, right alignment, and center alignment.

Vertical Alignment

For vertical alignment, you have bottom alignment, top alignment, and middle alignment.

But if you want to modify the text alignment of your border in cells, you can use these shortcuts:

- Press Alt + H then A + L for aligning the left side.
- Press Alt + H then A + R for aligning the right side.
- Press Alt + H then A + C for aligning the center.
- Press Alt + H then A + B for aligning the bottom.
- Press Alt + H then A + T for aligning the upper part.
- Press Alt + H then A + M for aligning the middle part.

Duplicating Cell Value

If you want to duplicate the value of the cell above the active cell, press Ctrl, Shift, and (which is actually since the key will be shifted).

Text Alignment Setting and Alt Shortcut Keys

If you want to change the text alignment of a cell, you can do so by performing multiple combinations of keyboard shortcuts. For example, if you want to align to the center, you must press and hold Alt. After that, press H, A, and C.

Technically, you are just using the Alt shortcut keys for the ribbon.

Pressing H after the Alt key will take you to the Home tab of the ribbon. Pressing A means that you want to toggle on the alignment toolbar buttons. And pressing C means that you want to activate the align center button. You can review the shortcuts for the alignment buttons by pressing the Alt key.

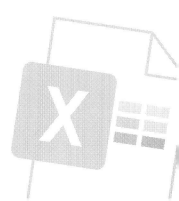

Chapter 4

HOW TO ENTER, EDIT, AND MANAGE DATA

Entering and Editing Data Manually

Entering Data

Click on a cell in the worksheet area and a rectangular box will appear around the cell. This is the *cell pointer* or the active cell. You can move the cell pointer with the left, right, up, or down arrow keys on your keyboard.

To enter data, simply type it directly into the cell or you can click in the formula bar and type the data there. To enter a formula, you need to prefix your entry with the equal sign (=).

Editing Data

When typing in the worksheet area, if you want to make a correction use the *BACKSPACE* key to go back and not the left arrow key. The arrow keys move the cell pointer from cell to cell. To use the arrow keys when editing data, select the cell and then click on the formula bar to edit the data there.

To overwrite data, click in the cell to make it the active cell and just type in the new value. This will overwrite the previous value.

If you only want to edit parts of the data in a cell, for example, a piece of text, then select the cell and click on the formula bar to edit the contents there.

Deleting Data

To delete data from your worksheet, select the data and hit the *Delete* key.

Default Content Alignment

In Excel, numbers and formulas are right-aligned in the cell by default. Everything else is left-aligned by default. So, you can tell if Excel recognizes your entry as a number or text value.

Using AutoFill

The Autofill feature in Excel enables you to fill cells with a series of sequential dates and numbers. It enables you to automate repetitive tasks as it is smart enough to figure out what data goes in a cell, based on another cell, when you drag the fill handle across cells.

Entering Dates with AutoFill

You may have a worksheet where you need to enter dates. You can enter **January** in one cell and use the AutoFill feature to automatically enter the rest of the months.

So, you first need to click on the cell to select it and then move your mouse pointer over the bottom right corner to display the small plus sign (+).

To AutoFill dates, enter **January** or any other starting month in one cell, then grab the small fill handle and drag it across the other cells.

AutoFill also works with abbreviations, but they must be 3 letters. For example, if you enter Jan and then drag down, it will be filled with Feb, Mar, Apr, May, etc.

Let's say you want to enter the 7 days of the week as your row headings. In the first cell of your range, enter **Monday** or **Mon**. Then drag the autofill handle down over the remaining 6 cells. This will AutoFill the remaining cells with Tuesday to Sunday.

Excel keeps the filled days selected, giving you a chance to drag the handle back if you went too far, or to drag it further if you didn't go far enough.

You can also use the *AutoFill Options* drop-down menu to further refine your fill options. To access the AutoFill options, with the cells still selected, you will see a drop-down button that appears on the last cell. When you click on it, you will get a list of options that enable you to select whether you want to copy the data across the cells, fill the series, copy formatting only, ignore the formatting, flash fill, etc**.**

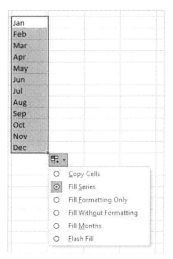

Note: If you don't see a button that enables you to access the AutoFill Options drop-down menu (shown above) after an autofill, it is most likely because the option hasn't been set in Excel Options.

To enable AutoFill Options (if it isn't available), navigate to:

File > Options > Advanced.

Under the *Cut, copy*, and *paste section*, select the checkbox for *Show Paste Options* button when content is pasted.

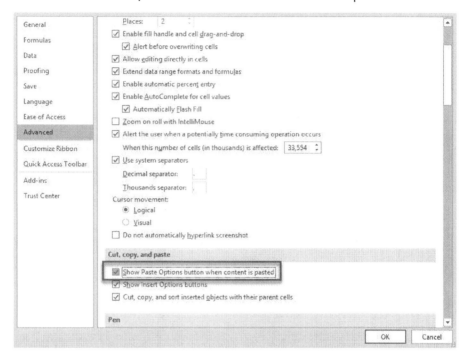

AutoFill Incremental Values

To AutoFill other incremental values, you need to first let Excel know what the difference is. So, you would need to enter values in at least two cells before dragging the fill handle across the other cells.

Let's say you want to enter dates that increment by seven days, i.e., a weekly interval. You would need to enter two dates (for example, 01/10/19 and 01/17/19). Then you select both cells and drag across the empty cells to autofill the other cells with dates having an interval of 7 days.

You can do the same with other numbers. If you enter 1 and then drag down, the number 1 will just be copied to the other cells. However, if you enter numbers 1 and 2 in two cells, and then select both cells and drag them down, you will get 3, 4, 5, 6, etc.

AutoFill the Same Values

To AutoFill the same value across a series of cells, enter the value in the first cell and then hold down the *CTRL* key while dragging the fill handle across the other cells.

For example, if you want to fill a range of cells with $6.99:

- Enter $6.99 in the first cell.
- Hold down the CTRL key.
- Move your mouse pointer to the bottom-right of the cell and grab the autofill handle (small square) and then drag it across the other cells.

Entering texts in Microsoft Excel worksheets

- Use of Auto Complete in Excel
- Adding or deleting cells in worksheets
- Entering a hyperlink in a worksheet
- Adding an outline for your data
- Use of Fill Handle in order to add data to cells
- Entering numbers and dates in Excel worksheets

A Microsoft Excel worksheet is very easy to understand. It is composed of columns and rows. Rows have been defined in numbers while the columns have letters. To enter data in a certain cell, you have to highlight it by clicking on it. The first cell, A1, is automatically highlighted, therefore if you do not make any selection, anything that you will type will appear on this particular cell.

The Cursor

The cursor in Microsoft Excel takes three important shapes that mean a different thing.

- The thick white cross is the one that you will use for cell selection
- The four-headed arrow will be used to move cells and other items in the worksheet
- The thin black cross will be used to fill in data automatically and also for copying formulas that you want to use.

Entering Text

To do this you will select the cell where you want to enter the text by clicking on it. Type in what you want to appear on that cell. You can also type data in the formula bar, especially if you are typing in a large text and it will automatically appear on the selected cell. If you want the same text to appear in more than one column, you drift the cursor over the columns of your choice and when they turn grey, drag the data that you have already typed.

Adding and Deleting Cells in Excel Worksheet

Adding and deleting cells is possible when you are working on a Microsoft Excel worksheet. In order to add a cell, highlight the cell where you want to add another cell and then right-click on it. From the drop-down menu that appears, select insert and this will bring you a dialog box from which you will select the kind of cell that you want to insert, then click ok.

To delete a cell, do the same thing but instead of selecting insert from the drop-down menu, select delete, then make a choice of what you want to be deleted and then click ok.

The Use of Auto Complete

Auto compete happens when you are typing data in a list. The program will try to guess what you are about to type depending on the data that you have typed in the previous cells. To type faster, you just enter if the guess is right.

Adding an Outline for Your Data

Outline in Microsoft Excel is used to group data. It helps a lot, especially if you want to limit the amount of data that you are viewing. There are two types of outlines in Excel; Manual and Auto. The Auto outline will be the best to use in the case of summaries. A Manual outline on the other hand will be perfect in case you only have a list and you want to choose groups.

In order to add an outline, click on the Data tab, then on the outline group, select the group of your preference from the drop-down menu. Choose auto outline. Now you can use + or – to enlarge or collapse the sections respectively on the side of your worksheet.

Adding a Hyperlink

How to Add Word Art to a Worksheet

If you are working with Excel 2013, you can easily insert word art in your Excel worksheet. Just go to the insert tab again, then select Word Art and you will have a variety of options to choose from.

Formatting Tables

You will be able to choose between dark, medium, and light options.

This option will also allow you to create your own style by selecting the more option after selecting Cell Styles.

Selecting New Table Style will allow you to name your style, before formatting using all of the formatting options available when formatting existing cells.

The Table Style Options grouping of options will allow you to turn headers on or off, turn totals on or off, determine if special formation is allowed and if alternating rows or columns will be alternating colors to make the table easier to read.

If you wish to format an already existing table, simply select the table in question before following the steps listed above.

Chapter 5

EXCEL WORKBOOKS DESIGN
OPTIONS

Starting a New Workbook

There are a few ways of starting a new workbook. First, you can start a new workbook by clicking on the blank workbook on the startup interface as shown below:

Another way of starting a new workbook is by clicking on the new icon on the interface or simply by pressing on your keyboard CTRL + N to open create q new workbook. The workbook interface is shown below.

Opening an Existing Workbook

To open an existing workbook, click Open Other Workbooks in the lower-left corner, then click Browse on the left side of the resulting window, then use the file explorer to find the workbook you wanted to open, select it, and click Open.

Working on Your Excel Sheet

Zooming in and Out Your Worksheet

To zoom in or out your worksheet, scroll to the bottom right side of your worksheet and click the plus button to zoom in and the minus button to zoom out.

Copying and Pasting of Data

You can copy and paste data either from one Excel cell/worksheet/workbook to another or from other applications on your computer to Excel. The copy procedure is still the same as normal copying of files or data, just highlight the data you wish to copy and click copy. In order to paste the data into your Excel worksheet, click the cell you want the pasted data to begin from, then right-click on the cell and select paste or simply press the shortcut key: CTRL + V.

Once you click the paste option, two basic options will be loaded asking you to select the format options you want, the first is the *keep source formatting;* what this paste option does is to keep the data format the same as from where it was copied, this will keep the data format constant with respect to the data source. The second option is the *match destination formatting;* what this does is that it will match the data to the current data format on your active worksheet.

Adding a New Worksheet

You can have numerous worksheets in a workbook. To add a new worksheet to your workbook, just navigate to the bottom-left of the workbook and click on the plus sign that's situated beside the sheet.

Renaming a Worksheet

A new sheet can be renamed simply by double-clicking on the sheet tab and entering the new name you wish.

Highlighting Numbers and Texts

To make Excel highlight cells automatically, choose the cells you want to apply conditional formatting to. Tap on the first cell within the range and drag it to the last cell.

Go to your worksheet and select the *Home button*. Tap on the *Conditional Formatting icon* and select *Highlight cells Rules*.

Move to the *Text that Contains section* and on the left side, click on the text you want to be highlighted.

After this, choose a color format for the text and tap on the *Ok icon.*

How to Transpose on your Worksheet

If you want to transpose or rotate data from columns to rows or rows to columns, follow these procedures:

a. Choose the range of data you want to rearrange.
b. You can also highlight rows and columns.
c. Then, tap on Ctrl + C buttons.
d. Navigate to a new location in the worksheet to paste the transposed data.
e. But ensure that there is enough space to paste your information.

Another way is to select the new cell where your transposed data will be copied. Right-tap on that cell and highlight the *Transpose button.* This is located under Paste.

Now, you can change the rows and columns using paste and transpose. Simply open the worksheet you want to change and tap on the first cell of your data range such as A1.

Then, you can shift-tap the last cell within the range.

Coloring a Worksheet

You can add colors to your worksheet by right-clicking the worksheet and selecting the color tab to make a choice of color.

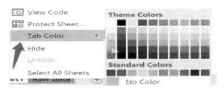

Saving Your File

To save your file, navigate to the File tab at the top-left side of the pane and select save. This will then launch you to a window where you can enter your file name and the corresponding folder; then click *Save*.

On the other side, you can also select the *Save as* an option, this will permit you to save a copy of your current workbook either with a new name or into a new folder.

Note: You can save your files either into your computer system or into your online drive. These options are available for both *Save* and *Save as* options. Saving into an online drive will launch you to your online drive.

Formatting Your Data

You can format your input data to your taste. First, we will be looking at how to format your data fonts. In the home tab under font options, there are various operations that you can perform on your input data varying from font size, font style, font color, and so on.

Formatting Font Style

You can alter your font style by selecting (highlighting) the data and clicking on the font pane to select the style you wish to use for the input data. Excel 2020 comes with a variety of good-looking fonts varying from Calibri to Arial to Verdana and so on.

Formatting Your Font Size

The font size of your data determines how big or small it will look on your worksheet. Depending on the type of document you are working on, you will have to choose your font size with respect to your desired output size. This means a bigger font size will provide a bold and big-looking data. To alter your data font size, first highlight the data you wish to change the font size, then navigate to the font size pane at the top left side of the worksheet, and toggle the font sizes to your choice.

In another way round, you can either increase or decrease your font size by clicking on the letter **A** that is situated just beside the font size pane. If you click the bigger **A,** it will increase your font size and if you click the smaller **A**, it will decrease the font size.

Formatting Number Type

There are times when you will be dealing with a particular number type such as currency. For example, if you are dealing with currency, different countries have different currency units and symbols. To insert a currency symbol into your input data, navigate to the number pane under the home tab and select the currency symbol you are dealing in.

Just in case the displayed currency type is not the currency you are dealing in, you can click the drop-down link beside the dollar symbol to load other currency types. One thing you will observe after choosing a currency type for your data is that decimal places will be input into your data.

You can choose to either increase or decrease the decimal place. To do this, click the zeros button beside the currency type. There are basically two buttons here, one is to increase the decimal places while the other is to decrease the decimal place.

Formatting an Overlap Data

Cells in Excel are designed with equal cell size by default.

There are times when you will enter data into a cell and it will overlap into the following cell, an example is shown below.

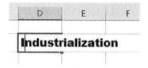

In the sample above, the data was entered into column D but as observed, the data has exceeded column D and has lapsed into columns E and F. To correct this, navigate to the top of the original cell column (column D in this example) and click the column, you will see that the column will be highlighted.

Once this happens, position your cursor at the extreme right edge of the column; then you will observe that the cursor will change to arrow-cross, then you can now click and drag the column edge until your data fit in.

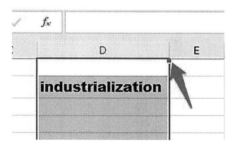

Another easier way you can do this is by highlighting the overlapped data cell and navigating to the format panel at the top-right side and selecting autofit column width (provided it overlaps by the width) or autofit column height (provided it overlaps by the height).

Repeating a Format Using the Format Painter

There are times when you would have performed a whole lot of formatting to a particular data and you will want to repeat the same formatting for different data entirely. Instead of going through the whole process and steps taken on the first data, you can make use of the format painter to repeat the formatting. To do this, highlight the formatted data, then double click the format painter button on the top-right side of the worksheet.

Once you double-click it, the previous formatting would have been activated and ready to be applied to any other part or data on the same worksheet. To apply the activated format, just click the cell containing the data you wish to apply the format to; immediately all the formatting will be activated to it.

Formatting Data into Table

There are times when you will have a range of data that you will love to format into a table. To do this, select the range of data you wish to format into a table.

Sample Data

OrderDate	Region	Rep	Item	Units	Unit Cost	Total
42375	East	Jones	Pencil	95	2	189.05
42392	Central	Kivell	Binder	50	20	999.5
42409	Central	Jardine	Pencil	36	5	179.64
42426	Central	Gill	Pen	27	20	539.73
				208		1907.92

Now navigate to the *format as table* in the style pane in the Home tab. A drop-down will show indicating different table formats, choose the one that best suits your data.

Once you select the table format, immediately a pop-up will show up requesting your confirmation of the cell involved. Click ok to proceed, then your data will be transformed into a table form as shown below.

Sample Data

OrderDate	Region	Rep	Item	Units	Unit Cost	Total
42375	East	Jones	Pencil	95	2	189.05
42392	Central	Kivell	Binder	50	20	999.5
42409	Central	Jardine	Pencil	36	5	179.64
42426	Central	Gill	Pen	27	20	539.73
				208		1907.92

Rotating Text Directions

There are times when texts directions need to be rotated to a specific angle. This is applicable mostly in tables, though it can also be done on pure data. To achieve this, select the cell containing the text you wish to rotate, after that navigate to the alignment pane under the Home tab and click on the arrow at the bottom right of the alignment pane to load more alignment options.

Once you click that button, the alignment extension will be loaded and you can now select the angle of your text rotation.

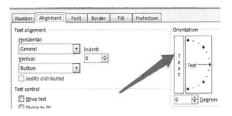

You can also choose to enter the rotation angle in the box.

Hiding and Unhiding Data

You can hide data and at the same time unhide data in Excel. To hide a range of data, highlight the cells this data belongs to and right-click on them and select hide.

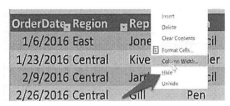

To unhide the data, just repeat the same procedure and select unhide and the whole data will become visible again.

Removing Duplicated Content from Excel Workbook

If you want to remove duplicates from Workbooks in Excel, follow these procedures:

1. Tap on any single cell within the set of data.
2. Navigate to the Data Tools section and click on the *Data menu.*
3. From the options, you can select *Remove duplicates.*
4. Ensure that you assess all *checkboxes.*
5. Then, tap on the *Ok icon.*
6. If you want to delete rows with identical countries and last names, examine the countries and last names you entered.
7. Then, click on the *OK button* to conclude.

Removing Duplicates without Deleting Rows

You can simply remove duplicates in a row without deleting the rows. This is done using filters. Click on a blank cell beside the data range such as D2. Enter a formula such as =A3=A2.

Choose all data ranges, including the formula cell. Tap on the *Data menu* and click on the *Filter icon.* This will activate the Filter function on your spreadsheet.

Another method to remove duplicates involves entering this formula =IF(LEN(TRIM(A1)) =0, ROW(), ''').

Now, A1 is the first data of the list you want to remove duplicates. Drag the AutoFill handle over the cells to get all the numbers of blank rows.

The Remove Duplicates tool permanently removes identical or repeated records. To avoid complications, you should copy or backup your data before deleting the duplicates.

Highlighting Cells with Formulas

Reviewing the rules for conditional formatting could be done in an active worksheet using the Quick Analysis tool. This will enable you to format the cells with duplicated text unconditionally.

But you can conditionally format cells in a row based on a text in one of the cells. Follow these steps to handle it:

1. Tap on the *Home menu* on the Ribbon.
2. Press on the *Conditional formatting icon.*
3. Select the *Manage Rules bar.*
4. Click on the Worksheet from the menu in the *Conditional Formatting rules Manager Section.* In this menu, every rule is labeled with its unique formula. They have peculiar ranges, formats, and checkboxes for Stop if True conditions.

Chapter 6

HOW TO ORGANIZE DATA
(ROWS AND COLUMNS)

Inserting a New Row and Column into Your Table

You may need to insert a new row or column or both into your table.

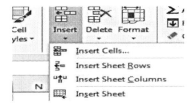

Select the insert sheet column and automatically the column will be added.

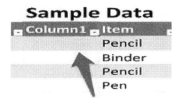

The same procedure goes for the row, if you wish to add a new row, follow these steps to get it done.

An easier and faster means of inserting rows and columns is by clicking the row or column where you wish to add a new one, then right-click and select insert. This will automatically insert a new row/column depending on your selection area.

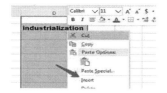

Naming Rows and Columns

Start by selecting the row or column you wish to rename.

View the naming options that can be found underneath the Formulas tab.

Select the name manager option, then edit to change the name of the row or column. The scope option will determine if the change will apply to the entirety of the workbook or just the current worksheet.

Defining Names

If you have included row or column names, these can be converted into table names.

Start by selecting the group of cells you want to be included under the name.

Select the Formulas tab and the Defined Names grouping of options before choosing the option to Create from Selection.

The resulting dialogue box will list any related labels that already exist and allow you to choose the one that will cover the entire table.

Creating names with the new name dialogue box:

Select the Formulas tab and the Defined Names grouping of options before choosing the Define name option.

Add the name and the scope (workbook or worksheet) of the name. This box will also allow you the opportunity to enter a descriptive comment relating to the name that will appear when you hover your cursor over the name.

In the box labeled Refers To, enter the cell or group of cells that the name refers to. Formulas can also be named in this fashion.

Managing Named Content

Select the Formulas tab and the Defined Names grouping of options before choosing the option labeled Name Manager.

This option will display all of the named ranges or tables that are in the current workbook. You can see names, values, what the name refers to, its scope, and any related comments.

You have the option on this screen to add new names, edit existing names, and delete names.

The button directly above the close button will highlight and show the cells the selected name refers to.

The name manager will not appear if you are currently editing a named range or table.

Creating Column and Row Headings

Select the Page Layout tab before choosing the Sheet Options selection.

From there you will be taken to the Page Setup dialogue box.

Underneath the list of options under Print, you will find the option to turn on Row and Column Headings.

Creating a Table

Start by selecting the data you wish to convert into a table.

Select the tab labeled Insert and select the option for Tables, then click the option for a single table.

If you have named individual rows and columns in relation to the range in question, make sure you select the option indicating My Table Has Headers; otherwise, these will be created automatically. Ensuring headers do not show at all can be done by right-clicking on the completed table, choosing the Design option, the Table Style option, and then deselecting the Header Row option.

Choosing the OK option will cause Excel to consider the first column as the header column and the first row and the header row for table creating purposes.

The Shortcut to Remove Blank Rows

If you want to remove blank rows using a shortcut, apply these steps:

1. Visit the *Home menu.*
2. Tap on the *Delete command.*
3. From the list, click on the *Delete Sheet rows icon.*
4. Another easy keyboard shortcut to delete columns, rows, and even cells is by tapping *Ctrl + -* using your keyboard.
5. Then, all the selected rows, columns, and cells will be deleted automatically.

Adding Several Rows in Excel

You can add multiple rows in Excel by selecting the row under where you want the new rows to be displayed. Go to the selected row and right-click on it. Choose the *Insert icon* from the menu.

Select the same number of rows you want to add if you want to insert multiple rows. Go to the selected cells and tap on the Insert icon from the list.

Another process is using shortcuts such as tapping on Alt-4 as many times as required. Then, add the first row by tapping Alt-4 once.

To repeat the action above, press *Ctrl + Y icons* or simply press F4. Now, you can choose multiple cells by pressing down the *Shift key* and using the Down arrow key in selecting multiple cells.

Inserting Multiple Rows

Inserting multiple rows in Excel can be done by selecting the row under the point you want the new row to show. Scroll to the highlighted row and right-tap on it. Go to the menu and click the *Insert button* from the options.

But if you want to insert multiple rows, choose the number of rows you want to insert. Then, you can right-tap within the selected section and tap the *Insert button* from the options.

Using a Shortcut to Insert Multiple Rows

If you want to insert multiple rows in an excel worksheet, here are the various options to use:

1. Enter Alt-4 as required.
2. Press Alt-4 once to insert the initial row.
3. Click on F4 or *Ctrl Y buttons* to repeat this action.
4. Press down the *Shift key.*
5. Select multiple cells using the downward arrow.

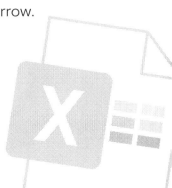

Adding Text to Columns

When you want to add text to columns in Microsoft Excel, use these procedures:

a. Launch Excel software.
b. Open a new blank workbook.
c. Enter texts to the first column.
d. Highlight all of them.
e. Go to the upper part of the ribbon and click on the *Data bar.*
f. From the list, tap on *Text to Columns.*
g. Click on Delimited and tap on the *Next icon.*
h. Scroll to the Delimiters menu and clear all the boxes.
i. You can also select comma and space.
j. Then, tap on the *Finish icon.*

Chapter 7

MOST USED FORMULAS AND CALCULATIONS TO SAVE TIME

Formulas are one of the key components that make Excel such an effective data storage and processing application. The large variety of formulas made available to the user allows complex data manipulation, processing, and handling routines to be easily introduced. Computational routines can be set up and adapted to large bulks of data with little modification.

Basic Formulas

So, what formulas are available to the Excel beginner user, and how can you employ them for maximum productivity? Excel's primary purpose is to perform calculations. From simple arithmetic to multifaceted expressions, these computations are inserted into a cell in the form of a *formula* or *function* and require the appropriate *syntax*.

Is there a difference between a **Formula** and a **Function**?

In Excel®, the terms *'formula'* and *'function'* are used interchangeably. Most users do not differentiate between the two. Even Microsoft® labels the tab *'Formulas'* when really it is more representative of functions.

The subtle difference is a *'function'* is entered with a *name*, such as *'SUM,' 'AVERAGE,'* or *'VLOOKUP'* and typically involves the evaluation of other cells. A *'formula'* may be entered with an operator like (+, -, *, or /) and does not require the inclusion of cells. Below is an example: **Formula: =2+2** result is 4.

Function: =SUM(B2:B3) result is 4.

	A	B
1	**Formula**	**Function**
2	2	2
3	2	2
4	=2+2	=SUM(B2:B3)

From a communication standpoint, it is much easier to say 'formula,' since this is what most people are familiar with. Therefore, in this book, the term 'formula' is used more often.

FUNCTION

A *function* in Excel® is a predefined formula. An example of a function name is 'SUM.'

FORMULA

A *formula* calculates numbers or evaluates the contents of one or more cells.

SYNTAX

> *Syntax* in Excel® refers to the arrangement or order of a formula or function. All formulas & functions begin with the equal sign (=) followed by numbers or the function's name.

Below are the fundamental formulas most people learn first.

ARITHMETIC APPLICATION	OPERATOR	DEFINITION
Sum (Addition)	+	Adds two or more cells or numbers together
Subtraction	-	Subtracts two or more cells or numbers
Multiplication	*	Multiplies two or more cells or numbers
Division	/	Divides two or more cells or numbers

Step-By-Step Examples

Sum (Addition)

Begin by creating a new blank Excel® spreadsheet:

From your keyboard, press shortcut keys *(CTRL+N) or*

Click the *'New Document'* icon from the *'Quick Access'* toolbar:

Enter the following numbers into *column 'A'*

Cell *'A1'* enter the number *2*

Cell *'A2'* enter the number *3*

Cell *'A3'* enter the number *1*

Cell *'A4'* enter the number *2*

The spreadsheet should look similar to the following:

	A
1	2
2	3
3	1
4	2
5	

Click cell *'A5'*

From the Ribbon select the tab *'Formulas'*

Click the Σ *AutoSum* drop-down arrow

Select Σ *Sum*

Press the *'Enter'* [Enter ←┘] button on your keyboard

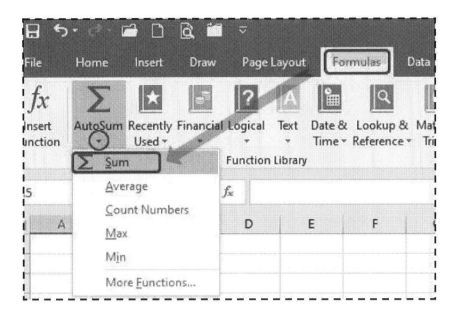

The result should be *8*:

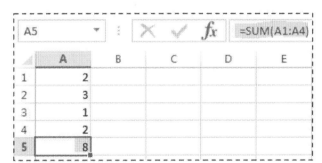

Alternatively, you may also type the following into cell 'A5':

Enter the *equal =* symbol from your keyboard

Type *sum(*

Select (highlight) rows *'A1:A4'*

Press the *'Enter'* [Enter ⏎] button on your keyboard

Subtraction

Using the same sample data as the 'Sum' section:

Select cell *'B3'*

Enter the *equal* = [+ =] symbol from your keyboard

Click cell *'A2'*

Enter the *minus -* [- -] symbol from your keyboard

Click cell *'A3'*

Press the *'Enter'* [Enter ⏎] button on your keyboard

	A	B
1	2	
2	3	
3	1	=A2-A3
4	2	
5	8	

The result should be *2*:

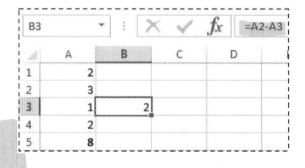

Multiplication

Using the same sample data as the 'Sum' section:

Select cell *'B4'*

Enter the *equal =* =̲/+ symbol from your keyboard

Click cell *'A4'*

Enter the *asterisk** *̲/8 symbol from your keyboard (shift key + 8 key)

Click cell *'A1'*

Press the *'Enter'* [Enter ←] button on your keyboard

	A	B
1	2	
2	3	
3	1	2
4	2	=A4*A1
5	8	

The result should be *4*:

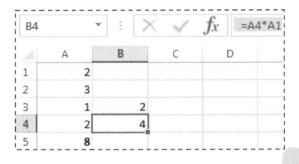

| B4 | | | X ✓ *fx* | =A4*A1 |

	A	B	C	D
1	2			
2	3			
3	1	2		
4	2	4		
5	8			

Division

Using the same sample data as the 'Sum' section:

Select cell *'C4'*

Enter the *equal =* 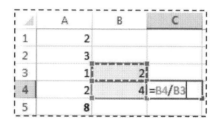 symbol from your keyboard

Click cell *'B4'*

Enter the *forward slash /* symbol from your keyboard

Click cell *'B3'*

	A	B	C
1	2		
2	3		
3	1	2	
4	2	4	=B4/B3
5	8		

Press the *'Enter'* 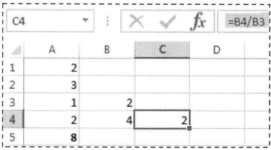 button on your keyboard

The result should be *2*:

| C4 | | | ⊗ ✓ ƒx | =B4/B3 |

	A	B	C	D
1	2			
2	3			
3	1	2		
4	2	4	2	
5	8			

Additional Examples

	A	B	C	D	E
1	ARITHMETIC APPLICATION	EXAMPLE DATA	EXAMPLE DATA	FORMULA	RESULT
2	Sum	2	3	=SUM(B2:C2)	5
3	Sum	-	-	=SUM(2+3)	5
4	Sum	-	-	=2+3	5
6	Subtraction	3	1	=B6-C6	2
7	Subtraction	-	-	=3-1	2
9	Multiplication	7	9	=B9*C9	63
10	Multiplication	-	-	=7*9	63
12	Division	4	2	=B12/C12	2
13	Division	-	-	=4/2	2

	A	B	C	D
1	ADDING NUMBERS TOGETHER	SUM & MULTIPLICATION	SUM & DIVISION	
2	2	2	2	
3	3	3	3	
4	7	7	7	
5	4	4	4	
6	=A2+A3+A4+A5	=SUM(B2:B5)*2	=SUM(C2:C5)/2	FORMULA
7	16	32	8	RESULT

Arithmetic Operators

The following arithmetic operators are used to perform basic mathematical operations such as addition, subtraction, multiplication, or division.

Arithmetic operator	Meaning	Example
+ (plus sign)	Addition	=4+4

– (minus sign)	Subtraction	=4–4
		=-4
	Negation	
* (asterisk)	Multiplication	=4*4
/ (forward slash)	Division	=4/4
% (percent sign)	Percent	40%
^ (caret)	Exponentiation	=4^4

Comparison Operators

Comparison operators allow you to compare two values and produce a logical result, i.e., TRUE or FALSE.

Comparison operator	Meaning	Example
=	Equal to	=A1=B1
>	Greater than	=A1>B1
<	Less than	=A1<B1
>=	Greater than or equal to	=A1>=B1
<=	Less than or equal to	=A1<=B1
<>	Not equal to	=A1<>B1

How to Enter a Formula

Once a cell is activated (clicked on and has a green box around it), a new formula can be inserted using the "formula bar" as shown below. Alternatively, you can type the formula directly into the cell provided you insert the character "=" first.

Arithmetic Operations

Arithmetic operations can be directly typed into a cell and the answer will be computed. For instance, you can type in a cell "=5+4*3" and it will show the result 17.

Copy and Paste Formulas

When copying and pasting from a cell that contains a formula, you must be very careful. After you copy a cell with a formula in it and you right-click on a new empty cell you will see different pasting options. You have two options:

Copy the formula into the new cell—this can be useful if used appropriately, however, keep in mind that if the cell contains any cells referenced, they will remain the same. If you are pasting to a new worksheet or file, these references will become errors and the formula will be invalid.

Copy the result of the formula into the new cell (what is displayed): this option ensures that no null reference errors are encountered. This option is recommended when copying across different worksheets or files.

Calculating Percentages

Let's say we want to calculate 20% of a value and then add it to the total, the way sales tax is calculated in invoices.

The price of the product is $2,900 and the sales tax is 20%.

Note: 100 percent is 1 in Excel, so, anything less than 100 percent will be less than 1. Hence, 20 percent will be 0.2. Always enter a percent as a decimal place number, unless it is 100% or greater.

For the *Sales tax,* we then enter 0.2 in cell B3.

We can format the cell as a *Percentage* (although this is not a must when calculating percentages in Excel). On the Home tab, in the Numbers group, click on the % sign. This will change the 0.2 to 20%.

For the *Price,* enter $2,900.

For the Sales Tax formula, enter **=A6*B3** to calculate 20% of $2,900, which is $580.00.

For the *Total,* you can use the AutoSum tool to generate the sum, or you can enter the formula directly **=SUM(A6:B6)** to produce the total figure of $3,480.00.

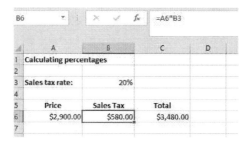

You can use the same method above to subtract percentages. For example, if we wanted to subtract the Sales Tax from the Price we would enter **=A6-B6** in cell c6.

Chapter 8

HOW TO USE THE DROP-DOWN LIST AND DATA VALIDATION

D ata validation is a spreadsheet feature that can provide you with the ability to create a list of specific entries that will then restrict what values you can place in each cell. You can also create a message elaborating on what types of data will be allowed in the cells, add warning when the wrong type of data is put into the cells, and check for cells filled with the wrong information through the use of the Audit function. Finally, you can set a range of specific values to be placed in any cell or determine this range based on the results of a different cell.

How to Insert Data Validation

To add data validation, follow the procedures below:

Select the cell you wish to validate.

From the **Data tab**, go to the **Data Validation button** and click on it.

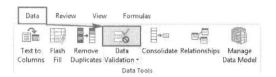

On the **Settings tab**, modify the validation criteria according to what you have in mind, and then click on **Ok.**

You can add an input message by clicking on the **Input Message** box to enter the title and text of your message relating to the field and click on **Ok.**

You can display an error alert by clicking on **Error Alert** and moving to the Style box to select the alert type. Then enter the title and text of the error message and then click on **Ok.**

Editing Data Validation in Excel

You can change the validation rule in Excel by performing the steps below:

Select any of the validated cells.

From the **Data tab**, go to the **Data Validation button** and click on it.

On the **Settings tab,** make the necessary adjustments.

Click on **Apply these changes to all other cells with the same settings** and then click on **Ok**.

Removing Data Validation in Excel

In case you change your mind about removing the data validation from your Excel worksheet, follow the steps below:

Select the cells with data validation.

From the **Data tab**, go to the **Data Validation button** and click on it.

On the **Settings tab**, select the **Clear All** button and then click on **Ok.**

Filtering Data in Excel

Filters in Excel are used to display and hide some data in your worksheet. You can filter your date, time, date, and numbers. To filter any data on your worksheet, follow the procedures below:

Click on the column of the header in the worksheet.

Go to the **Data tab** and click on **Filter**.

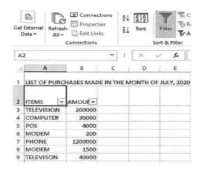

Click on the **Filter drop-down arrow** that appears on the header of the column.

Unmark the box you don't want in your worksheet.

Click on **Ok** and the data will be filtered.

Grouping of Data in Excel

Grouping data in Excel enables you to hide data from either the rows or columns. To group data:

Select the data you want to group.

Go to the **Data tab** and click on **Group.**

Select **Row** and click on **Ok.**

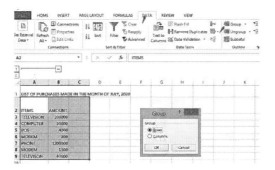

In the image below, the data in the cells are grouped.

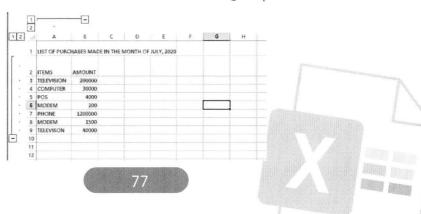

Creating Data Validation Rules

You can insert validation rules in cells to ensure that the data that is entered meets a certain criterion. For example, let's say we want to create a list that will be used by many people. The list has the following columns: **Product Code**, **Product Name**, and **Price**. We want to insert a validation rule to ensure the *Product Code is between 5 and 10 characters only*. We could also specify whether we want numbers only, letters only, or a combination of both.

For this example, we will make it a combination of letters and numbers.

Below is an example of how the list would look.

	A	B	C
1	Product Code	Product Name	Price
2	NWTB-1	Chai	$18.00
3	NWTCO-3	Syrup	$10.00
4	NWTCO-4	Cajun Seasoning	$22.00
5	NWTO-5	Olive Oil	$21.35
6	NWTJP-6	Boysenberry Spread	$25.00
7	NWTDFN-7	Dried Pears	$30.00
8	NWTS-8	Curry Sauce	$40.00
9	NWTDFN-14	Walnuts	$23.25
10	NWTCFV-17	Fruit Cocktail	$39.00
11	NWTBGM-19	Chocolate Biscuits Mix	$9.20
12	NWTJP-6	Marmalade	$81.00

How to Add a Data Validation Rule Select the cells for which you want to apply the rule.

Click on the **Data tab** in the Ribbon, and in the **Data Tools** group, you will find the **Data Validation** command.

Click on **Data Validation** to launch the Data Validation dialog box. The box has three tabs, **Settings, Input Message**, and **Error Alert**.

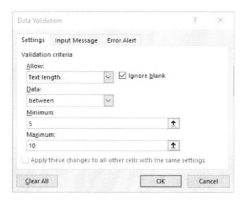

On the **Settings tab**, the **Allow** drop-down list gives us several options including, Text length, Whole number, and Decimal. In the **Allow** box, we choose **Text length**.

The **Data** drop-down list provides several comparison operators we can use in our validation criteria. For this example, we want the **Product Code** to be no less than 5 characters and no more than *10* characters.

So, for our validation criteria we'll enter these entries:

Allow: Text length

Data: between

Minimum: 5

Maximum: 10

On the **Input Message** tab, we add a **Title** and the **Input message**. This help message will be displayed as a small pop-up message when the user clicks on a cell with the validation rule.

For this example, we can add a message like: "The Product Code can be alphanumeric, and it should be between 5 and 10 characters."

In the **Error Alert** tab, we need to enter the message that is displayed when an entry fails the validation rule.

For the **Style**, we have 3 options. **Stop, Warning**, and **Information**. We will choose the **Stop** icon for this example, as a **Product Code** that does not meet the validation rule cannot be entered.

We can complete the **Title** and **Error Message** with the following: *Title: "Invalid Entry!"*

Error Message: *"Invalid entry. Please enter a value between 5 and 10 characters in length."*

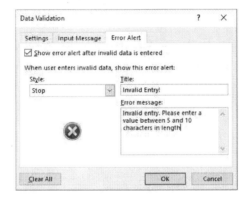

Once you have completed all the tabs, click *OK.*

Data validation will now be applied to the selected cells.

How to Edit or Remove Data Validation Rules

Occasionally you may want to change or remove data validation. To remove data validation, do the following:

Select the cells where data validation has been applied.

On the **Data** tab, click on the **Data Validation** command to launch the Data Validation dialog box.

To change the validation rule, simply edit the various entries and click **OK** when done.

To remove the validation rule, click **Clear All**.

Click **OK**.

Create a Dropdown List

Start by adding content to a worksheet in contiguous cells.

Assign a name to the data as if you were creating a table.

Select the cell that you wish for the drop-down menu to be connected to.

Choose the Data tab followed by the Data Validation option found in the Data Tools grouping.

Under the Settings tab look for the box named Source and enter the name of your list preceded by the = sign.

Under the Input Message tab enter a title and any additional message you want the drop-down list to display.

Check the box offering In-Cell Dropdown and select **OK**.

You can also include a variety of error alerts to prevent incorrect data from being entered into the cell.

When you click on the cell in question the new dropdown box should then appear.

Chapter 9

EVERYTHING ABOUT THE
NAMED RANGE

A Named Range is a group of cells in Excel that have been selected and given one name. After you give the selection a name, the whole range can now be referenced as one unit using that name in Excel formulas and functions. This is like a table with a name.

For example, we may have a list of contacts we would like to use in formulas. We could either use A1:G17 to identify the range of data or name the range "Contacts" and then use that name to reference the data from then on.

	A	B	C	D	E	F	G
1	Company	Last Name	First Name	Job Title	Address	City	State/Province
2	Company A	Bedecs	Anna	Owner	123 1st Street	Seattle	WA
3	Company B	Gratacos Solsona	Antonio	Owner	123 2nd Street	Boston	MA
4	Company C	Axen	Thomas	Purchasing Representative	123 3rd Street	Los Angelas	CA
5	Company D	Lee	Christina	Purchasing Manager	123 4th Street	New York	NY
6	Company E	O'Donnell	Martin	Owner	123 5th Street	Minneapolis	MN
7	Company F	Pérez-Olaeta	Francisco	Purchasing Manager	123 6th Street	Milwaukee	WI
8	Company G	Xie	Ming-Yang	Owner	123 7th Street	Boise	ID
9	Company H	Andersen	Elizabeth	Purchasing Representative	123 8th Street	Portland	OR
10	Company I	Mortensen	Sven	Purchasing Manager	123 9th Street	Salt Lake City	UT
11	Company J	Wacker	Roland	Purchasing Manager	123 10th Street	Chicago	IL
12	Company K	Krschne	Peter	Purchasing Manager	123 11th Street	Miami	FL
13	Company L	Edwards	John	Purchasing Manager	123 12th Street	Las Vegas	NV
14	Company M	Ludick	Andre	Purchasing Representative	456 13th Street	Memphis	TN
15	Company N	Grilo	Carlos	Purchasing Representative	456 14th Street	Denver	CO
16	Company O	Kupkova	Helena	Purchasing Manager	456 15th Street	Honolulu	HI
17	Company P	Goldschmidt	Daniel	Purchasing Representative	456 16th Street	San Francisco	CA

One of the benefits of using a named range is that the name is an absolute reference. When you create a formula with that name, you can copy and paste the formula in any part of your workbook, including different worksheets in the workbook, and the name will always point to the same group of cells.

Creating a Named Range

There are two ways you can create a named range:

Method 1

Click in the Name box (this is the box on the left side of the screen, just above the worksheet area) and enter the name for your named range.

Press *Enter* on your keyboard to save the name.

In the example below, I selected A1:G17 and entered "Contacts" in the name box to name that range. I can now use "Contacts" in place of A1:G17 in all formulas and functions in this workbook.

By default, when you create a Named Range, it will be available across all worksheets in that workbook.

Method 2

Select the cells you want to include in the named range.

Click on the Formulas tab on the Ribbon. On the *Defined Names* group, click on *Define Name*.

A dialog box will be displayed that allows you to enter the name. Leave the Scope field as Workbook (which is the default) if you wish to reference the name in different worksheets in the workbook.

Click *OK* when done.

Editing a Named Range

On the Formulas tab, click *Name Manager* (in the Defined Names group).

The Name Manager dialog box will be displayed with a list of all the named ranges and tables in the workbook.

On the list, select the named range you want to edit and click on the *Edit...* button.

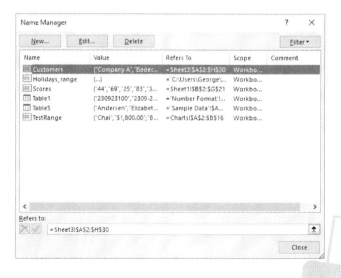

To change the area that makes up the range, click in the *Refers to* field. A scrolling marquee will appear around the current range. You can now select a new area or hold down the *Shift* key and adjust the current selection with your mouse pointer.

Click *OK* on the Edit Name box.

Click *Close*.

Deleting a Named Range

On the *Formulas* tab, click *Name Manager*.

Select the named range you want to delete from the list.

Click the *Delete* button.

Click *Close* when done.

How to Use a Named Range

To select a named range, click the drop-down arrow of the name box and select the name from the dropdown list. This will display the worksheet with the range (if you're on a different worksheet) and select all the rows and columns in the range.

For example:

The following example demonstrates the use of a named range called **Orders_Range** in place of the cell reference A1:D13. The example uses two formulas to count numeric values and blank cells in the range. The name of the range has been used as arguments in the functions instead of A1:D13.

=COUNT(Orders_Range)

=COUNTBLANK(Orders_Range)

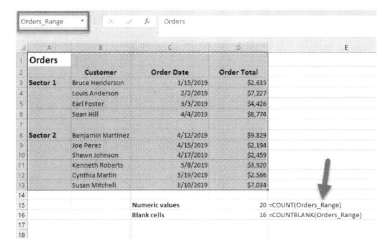

Chapter 10

HOW TO WORK WITH PIVOT TABLES

Pivot tables are an easy way to concisely compare large amounts of data. Your spreadsheet program is good about recognizing the need for pivot tables and, assuming your settings allow it, it will recommend the use of a pivot table and automatically create it if you let it, helping you to present, explore, analyze, and summarize your data as efficiently as possible. Before attempting to create a pivot table, it is important that you ensure all of your columns and tables have headings and that they are all free of unprintable characters/blank cells or extra spaces.

To insert a pivot table, begin by selecting a single cell that exists in the table or range of cells. From there, head to the Insert tab and then choose the option to let the spreadsheet recommend pivot tables. This will then open a new dialog box that will suggest a variety of pivot tables that could be made with your current data, choose the one you want, and the spreadsheet will create it as soon as you provide consent. Pivot tables can be deleted by simply selecting the pivot table in question and pressing the delete key. If you get an error message in response, ensure the complete pivot table has been selected and try again.

Create a Pivot Table from more Than One Existing Table

Relational data can easily be shown in a pivot table simply by grouping common values together. In these instances, the field list will show all of the tables you can show in the pivot table. The fields from each of these tables can then be placed on the table at your discretion. To use multiple tables from the same workbook you will first need to create a relationship between the two tables.

First, it is important that both tables have a column that can in turn be mapped to one of the columns from the other table. Ensure this column only contains unique information and both tables are named.

- Select the 'Data' tab and the option for 'Relationships' and then the 'New' option.
- Select the option for the base table that the other table or tables will then be linked to.
- In the Column Foreign option, choose the column that is relevant for the relationship.
- Select the table and column that you then want to relate to the first table and column in the Related Table/Column sections. Confirm your choices.
- Creating your pivot table should now result in multiple tables being visible on the pivot table field list option.
- Alter pivot table source data.
- Clicking on the pivot table you wish to alter will bring up the list of tools for use with the pivot table.
- Under the Data tab, select the Analyze option followed by Change Data Source.
- Select the new range you will want to use in the box labeled Table/Range. Instead of typing the new information, simply select it on your worksheet and it should auto-populate this section.

If your external data source has changed, this can be reflected from the same menu by selecting the external data source option.

Pivot tables based on data models cannot be changed.

Like regular tables, pivot tables can be refreshed by clicking on the pivot table you wish to refresh to bring up the tools for use with the pivot table, select the Data tab followed by the option to **Analyze**, then **Refresh** or **Refresh all** to refresh every pivot table in your workbook at once. You can also press the ALT key in conjunction with F5.

When altering data, ensure you select the prevent columns and cells from reformatting incorrectly by first selecting the Data tab followed by the option to Analyze and then **Options**. Select the tab labeled Layout and Format and ensure that the options for column width and cell formatting are selected.

Summarizing Data by Date

To display the columns split into years, drag a date field into the Columns box, for example, Order Date. The PivotTable tool will automatically generate PivotTable fields for Quarters and Years. Once these fields have been generated, you should remove the Order Date field from the Columns box and place it in the Quarter or Year field, depending on which one you want to use for your summary.

To display the row headings by date, place *Order Date* (or your date field) in the Rows box.

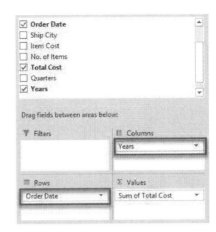

This will produce the following results.

Sum of Total Cost	Column Labels		
Row Labels	2016	2017	Grand Total
Jan	39569	7772	47341
Feb		22819	22819
Mar	5502	1854	7356
Apr	22724	57618	80342
May	3105	14510	17615
Jun	24021	596	24617
Jul	16060		16060
Aug	316	12141	12457
Sep	42763	9615	52378
Oct	16752		16752
Nov	34347	9756	44103
Dec	18896		18896
Grand Total	224055	136681	360736

As you can see, we can dynamically change how we want to view our data with just a few clicks. When you're happy with your summary, you can then apply formatting to the appropriate columns. For example, you could format *Sum of Total Cost* as *Currency* before any formal presentation of the data.

The good thing about PivotTables is that you can explore different types of summaries with the pivot table without changing the source data. If you make a mistake that you can't figure out how to undo, you can simply delete the PivotTable worksheet and recreate the PivotTable in a new worksheet.

Filter and Sort a PivotTable

On some occasions, you may want to limit what is displayed in the PivotTable. You can sort and filter a PivotTable just like you can do to a range of data or an Excel table.

To filter a PivotTable:

Click on the **AutoFilter** (down arrow) on the Row Labels cell.

The pop-up menu provides a list of the row headings in your PivotTable. You can select/deselect items on this list to limit the data being displayed in the PivotTable.

Uncheck *Select All*.

Scroll through the list and manually select the items you want to display.

Click *OK*.

The PivotTable will now show only the selected columns.

Applying a Custom Filter

You can also use the *Label Filters* and *Value Filters* menu commands to apply a custom filter to your PivotTable. This is done in the same way as you would do for a range or table.

Sorting PivotTable Data

To arrange the order of your data in a PivotTable, you use the same sorting methods you would use for a range or table.

Click on the *AutoFilter* button on the column named *Row Labels*.

Click on *Sort A to Z* (to sort in ascending order) or *Sort Z to A* (to sort in descending order). If your column headings are dates, then you'll get *Sort Oldest to Newest* (for ascending) and *Sort Newest to Oldest* (for descending).

Present Data with Pivot Charts

Another way you can present your pivot data is by using charts. A pivot chart is simply a chart based on a pivot table. So, instead of manually aggregating your data first before creating a regular Excel chart, you can simply generate a quick pivot table and pivot chart based on the pivot table. This makes the process much faster.

To create a pivot chart based on a pivot table, follow these steps:

Place the cell pointer anywhere in the pivot table.

Note that you can also find the *PivotChart* command button in the Tools group of the *PivotTable Analyze* tab (which is displayed on the Ribbon when the cell pointer is in the PivotTable).

Excel opens the *Insert Chart* dialog box that allows you to select the type and subtype of the pivot chart you want to create.

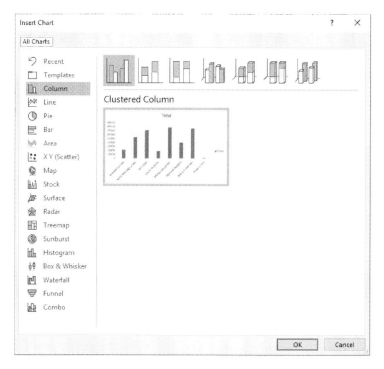

Select the type and subtype of the chart you want in the Insert Chart dialog box and click *OK*.

When you click OK, Excel inserts an embedded pivot chart in the worksheet with the pivot table used as the data source.

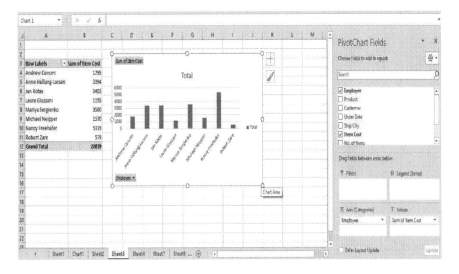

Tip: To move the chart around the screen, move your mouse pointer over the chart (the mouse pointer will change to a crosshair), then click and drag the chart to any part of the screen you want.

When you click on the PivotChart, three additional tabs appear on the Ribbon, *PivotChart Analyze, Design*, and *Format*. You can use commands on these tabs to redesign, modify, and format your pivot chart.

Filtering a Pivot Chart

After you generate a new pivot chart, you'll notice Field Buttons on the chart. These are dropdown list buttons for each of the fields represented on the chart. You can use these dropdown buttons in the pivot chart itself to filter what is represented on the chart in the same way you can do with the pivot table.

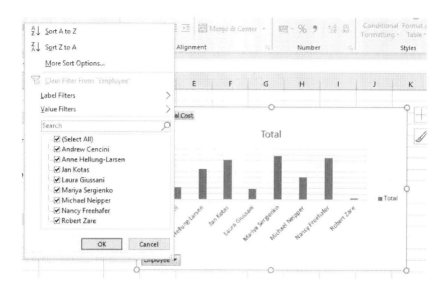

For our example above, we have the **Employee** drop-down button on the chart as that is the value being represented in the chart area.

To filter the chart, for example, if you want to exclude some names, you can click on the Employee dropdown button and uncheck *Select All*. Then you can individually select the names you want to represent in the filtered pivot chart.

To hide the Field Buttons on the chart, for example, if you want to print the chart without the buttons, do the following:

On the Ribbon, click the *PivotChart Analyze* contextual tab.

In the *Show/Hide* group, click *Field Buttons* (click the button's image rather than its drop-down arrow). You can toggle this button to show or hide the field buttons on the chart.

Moving the Pivot Chart

To move the chart to another worksheet, do the following:

Click on the pivot chart and then click on the *PivotChart Analyze* contextual tab.

In the *Actions* group, click the *Move Chart* command button. Excel displays the *Move Chart* dialog box.

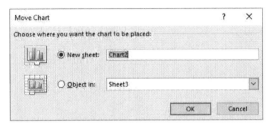

Select *New sheet* and in the corresponding text box, you can accept the default name provided for the new worksheet or type in another name of your choosing.

Click *OK* when done.

The pivot chart will be moved to a new worksheet.

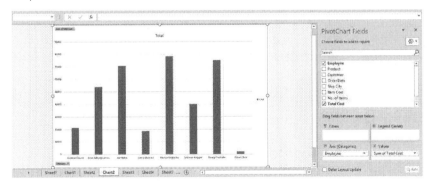

Generate a PivotTable and a PivotChart

You can generate a pivot table and a pivot chart simultaneously from your data list without having to generate the pivot table first.

To generate the pivot table and pivot chart together, do the following:

Click anywhere in the data list.

On the *Insert* tab click the drop-down arrow for the *PivotChart* command button.

Select *PivotChart & PivotTable* from the drop-down menu on the command button.

On the *Create PivotTable* dialog box, click the *OK* button.

Excel will create a new worksheet with the placeholders for a pivot table and a pivot chart. In the *PivotChart Fields* pane on the right side of the window, you can select the fields to go in your pivot chart, just as described in the section on manually creating a PivotTable in this chapter. As you select the fields you want for the chart in the PivotChart Fields pane, the pivot table and pivot chart will be created together.

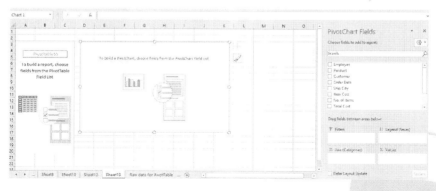

Chapter 11

ALL ABOUT CHARTS

A chart is a graphical or visual representation of data in a worksheet in such a way that the users can have a better understanding of the data rather than just looking at the numbers. Excel provides different kinds of chart formats that match what you want.

Types of Charts

Column Charts

Column charts are useful for data in both row and column forms. Column charts are ideal when you wish to show changes to data over time or wish to compare specific subsets of data. The average column chart places categories on the X-axis and values on the Y-axis.

Bar Charts

Bar charts are quite similar to column charts and share all the same subtypes. Bar charts are useful when it comes to illustrating how individual items compare to one another. When it comes to choosing between the two, consider a bar chart when working with durations of time as your values or when the axis labels are longer than average.

Line Charts

Line charts are a useful method of displaying data continuously over a specific amount of time. Typically, it is used to show how multiple variables performed along a set scale when compared to one another. Any data that is placed into rows or columns can be turned into a line chart and the X-axis holds category data and Y-axis contains the value data. Line charts are especially useful when various category labels are written as text and are spread out evenly such as quarters, months, or years.

Scatter Chart

Scatter charts are also able to change the scale of the horizontal axis to deliver a greater degree of specificity. It is also useful when you want to use a horizontal axis with a logarithmic scale, when the X values are easily segmented or when there are more than 10 points on the X-axis. It is also a great choice when you want to display numerous data points where time is not a factor. To prepare data for being put into a scatter chart, it is important to place all of the values that you want to be graphed on the X-axis in a single column or row and then enter the Y-axis values in the next column or row.

Pie Chart

For data that can be expressed in a single column or row, the best choice to display it visually is typically a pie chart. Pie charts are typically used to show individual parts of a whole in relation to the combined total of all of the parts in question. The percentage of each category's contribution will also be displayed as a percentage. Pie charts are the perfect choice when none of the relative values are negative, none of the values are zero, there are no more than seven categories being graphed and, most importantly, all of the values are related to a larger whole.

Area Charts

Area charts are useful for making the magnitude of a category's values change over time more readily visible. They are also an easy way to emphasize each value in relation to the whole. Area charts typically show a variety of plotted values as well as their sum total.

Customizing Charts

After creating a chart, you have several tools available for formatting and customizing the chart to your liking. For example, you can swap the axis, change/adjust the data source, update the chart title, adjust the layout, apply a chart style, and apply a theme color to your chart.

To demonstrate some of these options, let's say we need to create a chart with four quarters of sales.

	A	B	C	D	E
1	Sales by Quarter				
2	Product	QTR1	QTR2	QTR3	QTR4
3	Chai	300	300	200	400
4	Beer	300	200	400	300
5	Coffee	350	400	500	500
6	Green Tea	250	150	100	300
7	Tea	100	400	100	500
8	Chocolate Biscu	320	200	100	300
9	Scones	250	500	200	100
10	Brownie Mix	350	400	550	200
11	Cake Mix	200	370	300	200
12	Granola	250	100	200	400
13	Hot Cereal	350	500	300	200
14	Chocolate	350	200	500	500
15	Fruit Cocktail	200	230	250	200
16	Pears	100	200	300	450
17	Peaches	200	300	200	600
18					

To create the chart:

Select the range with the data, including the column headers and row headers.

Click on *Insert > Recommended Charts.* You're presented with the *Insert Chart* dialog box with several chart recommendations for your data.

Select the *Clustered Column* option.

Click *OK*.

A chart will be created and added to your worksheet.

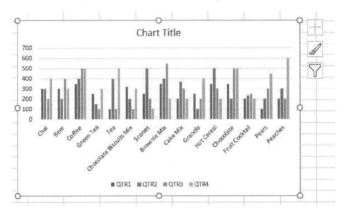

Switching the X and Y Axes

You can switch the values Excel applies to the vertical axis (also called the Y-axis) and horizontal axis (also called the X-axis).

To switch the values applied to the axes:

Select the chart.

Click *Chart Design > Switch Row/Column.*

This will swap the values applied to the vertical and horizontal axes.

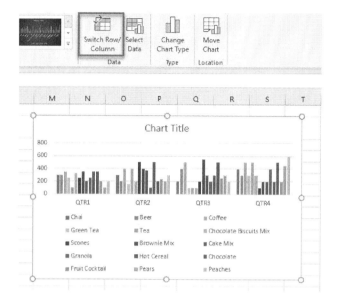

To swap the values back, simply click the *Switch Row/Column* button again.

Change the Data Source

To change the data used as the source of the chart, do the following:

Click the *Select Data* button on the *Design* tab. The *Select Data Source* dialog box will be displayed.

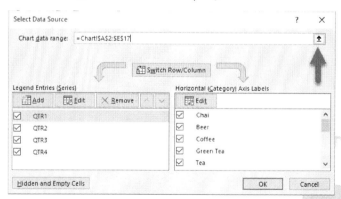

Select the up arrow that is on the *Chart data range* field. This will change it to a down-pointing arrow.

Select the cells you want in the worksheet area and click on the down-pointing arrow to return to the *Select Data Source* screen.

Click **OK** to confirm the change.

The new data source will now be used for the chart.

Adding Axis Titles

When you create a new chart, you'll see "Chart Title" as a placeholder that needs to be edited with the title of the chart. There are also no labels at the axis, and we may want to add them to the chart.

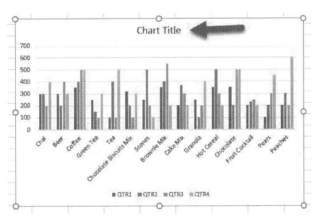

To change the *Chart Title,* you can simply click on it and type in the title. Alternatively, you can select the name from a field on your worksheet. For example, if we wanted our chart title to be **Sales by quarter,** which is in cell *A1* of our worksheet, we would click on the Chart Title label and in the formula bar, enter "=A1". This will use the value in cell A1 for our chart title.

We can also add titles down the left-hand side and at the bottom of the chart. These are called axis titles. The left side is the Y-axis while the bottom is the X-axis.

To change the layout of your chart, click on *Chart Design >
Quick Layout.*

You'll get a pop-up with several chart layouts. With the chart
selected, you can mouse over each layout to view more
details about it and get a preview of how your chart will look
with that layout. A few of the options provide axis titles as
well as move the legend to the right of the chart. If you want
a layout with both axis titles, then *Layout 9* would be a good
pick.

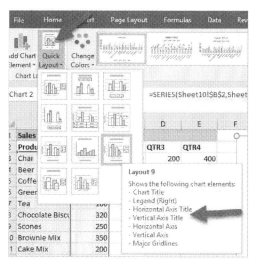

If we select *Layout 9*, we get a chart with labels that we can
edit to add titles to the X-axis and Y-axis.

You can edit the axis labels as described above. You can click
on the labels and type in the text directly or pull the text from
your worksheet area by typing in a cell reference, for example,
=A1, assuming cell A1 as the text you want for that label.

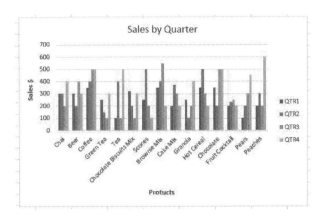

Chart Styles

When you click on the chart, the *Chart Design* tab shows up on the Ribbon. On this tab, you have an array of *Chart Styles* you can choose from to change the look and color of your chart.

To change the color of the plot area:

Click on the plot area to select it (this is the center of the chart) and it will be selected.

With the plot area selected, click on the *Format* tab on the Ribbon.

Click the drop-down button in the *Shape Styles* group.

You'll get a pop-up with many *Theme Styles* to choose from for the format of the plot area. You can mouse over each one to see a preview of how your chart would look like if selected.

When you find the one you like, click on it to select it.

Creating Sparkline Charts

Adding a Sparkline

Select the data you want to create a Sparkline chart for. At the lower-right corner of the selection, you'll see the *Quick Analysis* tool.

Click on the *Quick Analysis* tool to open a pop-up menu of Quick Analysis options—*Formatting, Charts, Totals, Tables,* and *Sparklines.*

Click on *Sparklines* and then select one option from *Line, Column,* or *Win/Loss.*

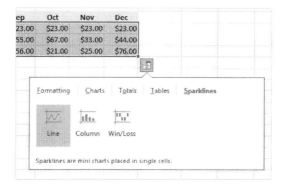

For this example, the *Line* option was selected. The sparklines will be created in the cells immediately to the right of the selected values.

To format your Sparkline chart, click on it to select it.

On the Ribbon, click on the *Sparkline* tab. In the *Style* group, you'll see various options to edit and style your sparkline chart.

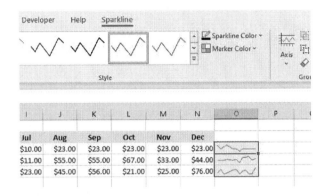

Use the following options to design your sparkline:

On the Sparkline tab, click on *Line, Column,* or *Win/Loss* buttons to change the chart type.

You can check *Markers* to highlight specific values in the Sparkline chart.

You can select a different *Style* for the Sparkline.

You can change the *Sparkline Color* and the *Marker Color.*

Click on *Sparkline Color > Weight* to change the width of the Sparkline.

Click on *Marker Color* to change the color of the markers.

Click on *Axis* to show the axis, if the data has positive and negative values.

Add/Remove Chart Titles

Adding titles to charts and individual charts X and Y axes provides an easy way to make complex information more readily apparent. Title options can be found under Chart Tools once a chart has been selected to allow access to the Format, Layout, and Design tabs.

To add a title to a chart, select the Layout tab and the grouping of options titled Labels to find the Chart Title option.

A box will appear labeled Box Title, fill it in and determine where you want the title to be placed.

Text formation options will appear once the text is highlighted; traditional formatting options will also be available.

To add titles to the axes, start by selecting the preferred chart and then viewing the Layout tab, the Labels grouping of options, and the option labeled Axis titles.

This option will provide you with the opportunity to label all the axes including multiple X or Y axes. To add a title for the Z-axis, select the option labeled Depth Axis Title.

Enter a title and you will be provided with formatting options as well.

Adding Data Point Labels

Individual labels can be added to specific data points in some charts to emphasize specific areas of importance.

To add a single label to all data points in a specific series or a single point in a series, start by selecting the desired chart to pull up the Chart Tools option.

Select the layout tab, followed by the Labels grouping of options and the option for Data labels.

This will provide you with options when it comes to naming an individual or multiple labels as well as removing unneeded labels.

Add a Legend

A legend is a quick and easy way to ensure that everyone viewing your chart knows exactly what they are looking at.

To add a legend to a specific chart, start by selecting the desired chart to pull up the Chart Tools option.

Select the Layout tab and the grouping of options titled Labels to find the Legend option.

Select the options related to your specific graph, additional options are available under the More Legend Options button.

Legend adjustments can be made through this window or by dragging the legend using the mouse. Adjustments made through the options menu will automatically populate and make adjustments to data placing as needed.

Selecting the legend and hitting the delete key will remove the legend from the chart.

Selecting the individual legend entries will allow you to edit them individually.

Modify Chart Size

Charts can be moved or resized by simply dragging them as required.

Charts can also be resized from the Format tab by selecting the Size grouping of options, then Shape Width, and Shape Height.

Additional options are located in the same place on the ribbon under the button next to the Size label. Here you will be able to determine if you want the chart to scale, rotate, or be resized.

The properties tab provides controls regarding how the chart moves in relation to how cells are resized in the worksheet.

Create a Chart Template

Start by selecting the chart that you will want to save for future use.

Select the Design tab and look for the grouping of options labeled Type and choose the Save as Template option.

By default, after you enter a name for the template, it will be viewable under the Templates option in the Insert Chart menu.

Giving the template a name and saving it will populate future charts with all of the colors, format, and height and width specifications as the original. It can then be modified as normal.

The template will be available across worksheets and workbooks.

Chapter 12

NEW FEATURES IN EXCEL
FOR 2021

Microsoft Excel 2021 is an easy-to-understand tool and with a lot of satisfaction. This new version has been transformed to a greater extent and new features have been as well updated to make your way of working easier.

One of these new features is the new Ribbon framework is much more instinctive and inevitably numerous clients come to incline toward this new route framework.

Now let's talk about a few of its features that have made it relevant, especially at this time.

Password Protection

Excel allows you to protect your workbook from unauthorized users from accessing your information by allowing you to create a password.

Data Filtering

The data filtering tool is a quick and easy way to locate and work with a set of data within a range. A filtered range only shows the rows that meet the criteria specified for a column. There are two commands available in Excel for filtering range, which are **AutoFilter** and **Advanced Filter.**

Data Sorting

Data sorting is a process of arranging data in a particular logical order. With Excel, you can sort out data in your worksheet either in ascending or descending order.

Built-In Formulae

One of the major operations carried out in Excel is the use of formulas to solve certain problems. With the consciousness that there are some works that can be done faster with formulas, Excel is installed with some formulas that are always coming in handy, some of them are SUM, MIN, MAX, AVERAGE, COUNTIF, COUNTA, TRIM, etc.

Creating Different Charts

Excel allows you to create different charts, such as line graphs, pie charts, bar graphs, *etc.*, to illustrate your data in such a way that can be understood easily.

Automatically Edits Results

Excel automatically edits results if any change or correction is made in the cell.

File and Replace Command

Excel allows you to find any data you need whether texts or numbers in the worksheet and replace them with a new one.

Conditional Formatting

One of the important features of Excel is used to change the format of the cell. With this feature, you can use the basic font and cell formatting tools such as font color, number font, cell borders, cell fill color, etc. You can also change the format of your graphical display of data even with this same feature.

Paste Special

While using the copy and paste feature in Excel, you may end up copying the format or formula you don't need when in reality, you only need the value, to avoid this, the paste special feature allows you to bring over the elements of the copied cells rather than copying the format along with it.

Flash Fill

While on the worksheet working on a task that follows the same sequence, Excel allows you to select the entire range of the cells by pressing **Ctrl+E** and then apply the action to the entire range.

Shortcut Keys

This is a feature of Excel that allows you to carry out some operations by just pressing two or three keys altogether. The following are good examples of the Shortcut keys:

✓ Ctrl + E - Flash fill

✓ Ctrl + A – To highlight all

Hyperlink

The Hyperlink function in Excel allows you to create the shortcut of a file or website address for easy access. To locate a hyperlink, click on the **Insert tab**, in the **Links group,** and then select **Hyperlink.**

Transpose

This is a function in Excel that allows you to change the direction of a range of cells to another. A good example is when a range of cells is inputted horizontally and now returns to vertical.

TRIM

Excel has another feature that allows you to remove extra spaces from the worksheet and this is known to be the TRIM function.

Sparklines

This is also another feature of Excel that allows you to create a mini-graph inside a cell.

Remove Duplicate

Some data may appear twice on your worksheet, making it difficult to work with. To solve this issue, all you need to do is use the Remove Duplicate feature in Excel to eliminate any repetitive data in the workbook.

Microsoft Excel and the Office Suite have almost infinite applications. Consider the following top ten list of Excel's most common and strong built-in features:

- Model and interpret virtually every piece of data more efficiently.
- Quickly zero in on the best data points.
- In a single cell, make a data chart.
- You can use your spreadsheets from almost anywhere.
- When people work together, they will connect, share, and achieve more.
- Take advantage of Pivot Charts that are more social and creative.
- Get the data presentations more sophisticated.
- Get it simpler and quicker.
- Increase the computing resources to create larger, more complicated spreadsheets.
- Excel Services allows you to publish and distribute your work.

When you combine this with the ability to configure and simplify every process using Visual Basic for Applications (VBA), you have a powerful BI (Business Intelligence) framework that is flexible and innovative enough to address almost any business need.

Do you want to use Microsoft Excel for your enterprise solutions? It would help if you depended on the Excel Help experts. We've worked with companies of all sizes and in a variety of industries. We will help you optimize your business processes with Microsoft Excel and other Microsoft solutions, whether you're a household name or a small business.

Other Operations in Excel 2021

Here are some of them:

1. **Adding a row**—to add a row, go to the **Row header** under where you want to insert a new column. Right-tap on any cell in the selected row. Tap on Insert from the options to add it to the system.
2. **Entering formulas**—tap on the cell where you want to enter a formula and type in the formula.
3. **Removing a Row or column operation**—select the entire row or column you want to delete. Go to the selected row or column and right-tap on any cell. Then, tap on Delete from the options.
4. **Adjusting the width of Columns**—select an entire column by tapping on the column header. Scroll to the highlighted area and right-tap on any cell. Press on the column width and enter a value for the column width from the menu.
5. **Showing Formulas within the worksheet**—press down the Ctrl key and tap the left single quote button. After this, come back to numbers by repeating this operation.
6. **Adjusting the row height**—tap on the Row header to

select the whole row. Select any cell on the highlighted section and right-tap on it. Scroll to the menu and click on Row Height. Enter a value for the row height. You can adjust the row height of different rows at the same time by clicking on multiple rows.

7. **Sorting operations**—tap on the grey rectangle between the *A column header* and the *I row header*. These are located on the top left side of the worksheet. With these actions, you can highlight the whole worksheet. Go to the menu bar and tap on Data. Locate the *Sort function* and from the options, click on *Sort by.* Choose the column to sort by and click on either the Descending or Ascending order.

8. **Arithmetic precedence**—the rule of arithmetic precedence is followed when evaluating formulas. These include the + / -, * and /, ^, and ( ).

- + / - are examined from the left to right.
- ^ this is called exponentiation.
- ( ) enclosed operations within parentheses are examined before others. Again, nested parentheses are examined inside out.

9. **Adding a column**—move to the Column header at the right side of where you want to insert a new column. Right-tap on any cell in the selected area. Hit on the Insert button from the list on the screen.

10. **Pasting columns, rows, and cells**—you can go to the Windows clipboard and choose the row, columns, and cells where you can paste texts already copied from your worksheet.

11. **Justifying an entire column or row**—press the row header or column. This will enable you to select them. Tap on the Justification menu and choose left Justify,

Right justify, or Center. This is located on the *Formatting Toolbar.*

12. **Adjusting the Format of Numerical Data**—tap your cursor and drag it over the cells having the numerical data. Go to the selected area and right-tap on any cell. Press Format Cells and tap on the *Number icon.* From the menu, click on Category. This will enable you to choose the type of data on the cells. You can also adjust the number of decimal places in numerical data by clicking on Number and typing the number of decimal places to use.

13. **Copying rows, columns, and cells**—highlight the cells, columns, and rows by selecting them. Scroll to the highlighted section and click on any cell. Tap on the *Copy icon.* You will see the highlighted cells transferred to the Windows clipboard transparently.

14. **Justifying the contents of cells**—tap on the cell and press on the Justification menu. Select Right Justify, Left Justify, or Center. This is located on the Formatting Toolbar.

Future of Excel

What are our choices now? With the internet playing such an important role in our lives and businesses, it's only natural that the interests of the many would win out. Staying current on new technology has been a full-time task as Microsoft platforms begin to grow. Microsoft Excel will continue to be the most popular framework for analyzing results, creating charts and presentations, and integrating with computer features for digital dashboards and business intelligence workflows.

Businesses are increasingly turning to cloud storage for data connectivity and collaboration. We see Microsoft Excel's future in the next few years advancing at a breakneck pace to have multi-user access to vast data for research, monitoring, and significant improvements in performance and productivity.

Custom solutions are expected in today's dynamic market climate to retain a competitive advantage and maximize income. Microsoft Excel consulting firms are the most knowledgeable on current and new developments. Having a retained specialist consultant is critical to achieving the maximum strength and efficiencies needed to succeed in the twenty-first century.

Chapter 13

EXCEL FOR ACCOUNTING—10 EXCEL FUNCTIONS YOU NEED TO KNOW

Accounting

Budgeting, forecasting, cost monitoring, financial reporting, loan calculators, and other tools are all accessible. Excel was essentially created to satisfy these various accounting requirements. And, given that 89 percent of businesses use Excel for multiple accounting functions, it clearly meets the criteria.

Excel also comes with a variety of spreadsheet models to help you with both of these tasks.

Excel is undoubtedly the most popular program in its category. It is widely used by many people in so many places across the globe. Excel is used in industries, amongst students, in general offices, and so on, and this makes it one of the best software programs that one needs to master in order to fit in a job setting today. When you are looking for a job, knowledge of the Excel program can easily place you in a better place than a candidate that has not mastered the basics of Excel. There are so many reasons why Excel is good for you, and some of these are:

Excel Is a Problem-Solving Program

Excel is known as a spreadsheet program, but at its very core, it is designed to solve mathematical programs. You need to know how much you can do with Excel in order to enjoy its full usefulness. When it comes to text data, for instance, Excel can solve any issue you might have; for instance, reconciliations, preparing PowerPoint presentations, and also sending emails to a big list of recipients.

Excel Will Save Your Time

Time is always needed in order to do more every day. Time is precious, hence you need to use the time that you have properly to avoid regrets afterward. Excel is a program that will make working easier for you and help you solve so many problems with ease. If you are looking for a certain piece of information, for instance, tracing it from an excel spreadsheet will be much easier than a lengthy word program. If you want to enter data faster, you will do it so well in excel. Much of the work is automated in Excel, thus you will only be required to enter just one piece of information and the rest will automatically be done for you.

Formatting Options

Businesses may use a variety of styling options, such as italics, highlighting, and colors, to make the most relevant data stand out from the others. This tool will perform a variety of functions, including whole row highlighting comparing lists and values, to name a few. You may use them to attract attention to specific Accounting entries.

Chart & Graphs for Analysis

You'll need to draw charts if you operate in a big organization where the manager needs a detailed visual description of the different market sectors. It's easy to do with MS Excel!

Organize All of Your Data in One Place

Excel enables you to build spreadsheets larger than 20 A1 documents, with over 1,048,576 rows and 16,384 columns in each spreadsheet, and hundreds of them, or more if your PC is able, in a single file! Via the insert tab, you can easily import from other spreadsheets and add pictures and other items, making it simple to get all of the data you've gathered from different files into one location.

It Boosts Productivity and Increases Performance

Yes, as previously said, advanced Microsoft Excel preparation will enhance employee performance and productivity, resulting in increased efficiency and productivity for the organization. The most productive your staff perform, the faster jobs and assignments can be completed, enabling you to offer greater support to your consumers and partners while still doing more work in a shorter amount of time. Even if the advantages of advanced Excel training save your employee a half-hour per week, when multiplied by the number of workers in the organization or business, that will add up to a large sum of additional staff hours per week.

It Enables You to Increase Employee Knowledge with Minimal Cost and Effort

Employees in your Business are now trained in the initial Excel program, and introducing basic training plans to help you to properly utilize the program will be far less costly than having to train new recruits in the company's processes and procedures, who also have experience of these specialized methods. Furthermore, advanced training may be easy, requiring just a few weeks or less for workers who have already shown intermediate proficiency. Instead of engaging in outside preparation facilities for an employee, you can save costs by employing an onsite trainer who can teach a significant part of the employees at once. It results in a more trained and professional workforce at a lower rate.

It Can Boost Your Career Development

Employees that are valued focus on acquiring new skills that will allow them to not only succeed in their current role but also advance up the corporate ladder. If you don't feed this need to learn, your employees' work satisfaction will suffer, and they will be less motivated to pursue their career path in your company. When you train workers, you increase their value to the business while also reducing turnover and giving the best employees an incentive to stay.

Increasing Your Productivity and Efficiency

When working with massive amounts of data and estimates, Excel is a vital method for increasing efficiency and enabling employees to be more productive. When you have a deeper understanding of Excel, you will be able to utilize its more powerful software, which will help you to complete assignments and interpret data more easily. It will also enable you to keep team members informed about data, which will help to speed up the workflow process.

Making You a Better Data Organizer

Spreadsheets are a popular method for gathering and organizing data. Excel is a spreadsheet program in the most basic form. It helps you to systematically organize all of your data while still allowing you to sort the information in whatever manner you choose. Data in its raw state can be confusing and difficult to understand. With Excel's advanced features, you'll be able to better organize the data, perform calculations as required, and filter the data so that it can be properly interpreted and converted to charts or graphs for better viewing.

Chapter 14

HOW TO MAKE CHECKLIST IN EXCEL

D o you want to increase your productivity? Excel will come to the rescue with a multitude of functions that can help you manage your activities and to-dos with comfort and organization.

- Task List
- Check List
- Project Management Charts
- Time Logs

Now, we discussed the above points, which are as given below.

Task List

Say goodbye to the old-fashioned to-do list on paper. With Excel, you can create a much more comprehensive task list—and also track your performance on the bigger tasks you already have on your plate.

TASK LIST

MY TASKS	START DATE	DUE DATE	% COMPLETE	DONE	NOTES
[Task]	[Date]	[Date]	0%		
[Task]	[Date]	[Date]	50%		
[Task]	[Date]	[Date]	100%	●	

Checklist

Similarly, you should make a quick checklist to cross off the items you've bought or completed—from a shopping list to a list of to-dos for a future marketing campaign.

PURCHASED?	GROCERIES:	
☐	Apples	
☐	Tomatoes	
☐	Milk	
☐	Eggs	
☐	Cheese	
☐	Bread	

Project Management Charts

Excel is a complete beast when it comes to making charts, as we've already said. This principle is often true when it comes to different project management charts.

Excel will help you maintain your project on track in a variety of ways, from waterfall charts to Kanban-style boards (like Trello) to monitor your team's progress.

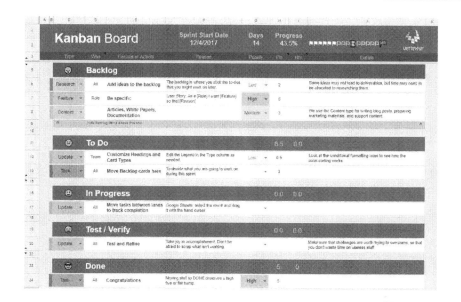

Time Logs

You also realize that keeping track of your time will help you be more productive. Although there are several fancy applications and software to help you fulfill the need, think of Excel as the initial time-tracking application. It continues to be a viable alternative today.

Time Sheet

[Employee name] | [Email] | [Phone]
Manager | [Manager name]

Period [Start date] - [End date]

Standard Work Week	Hours Worked	Regular Hours	Overtime Hours
40.00	0.00	0.00	0.00

Date(s)	Time In	Lunch Start	Lunch End	Time Out	Hours Worked
[Date]	[Time In]	[Lunch Start]	[Lunch End]	[Time Out]	0.00
[Date]	[Time In]	[Lunch Start]	[Lunch End]	[Time Out]	0.00
[Date]	[Time In]	[Lunch Start]	[Lunch End]	[Time Out]	0.00
[Date]	[Time In]	[Lunch Start]	[Lunch End]	[Time Out]	0.00
[Date]	[Time In]	[Lunch Start]	[Lunch End]	[Time Out]	0.00

Chapter 15

EXCEL FUNCTIONS YOU
NEED IN 2022

Some of the basic Excel functions and their descriptions include:

The Mod Function and How to Use it

After division, the Mod function in Excel returns the remainder of two numbers. Therefore, the outcome of MOD bears the same sign as the divisor number. Then, MOD (10,3) = 1.

This function is based on the Math and Trigonometry functions. It is regarded as the modulo operation. You can also call it modulus. This gives it the name MOD.

The Round Function and How to Use it

The Round function returns a number rounded to a given number of digits. It could be rounded to the left or right of a decimal.

The purpose of rounding numbers is to a specific number of digits. In this case, the return value is the rounded number. Therefore, the syntax is =ROUND (number, num, digits).

In this syntax above, the argument is that *number* is the number to round while num_digits is the number of digits that you want to round your numbers.

If you want to round numbers, it is advisable to use the round functionality. Apply the MROUND function when you want to round to the nearest multiple.

Also, apply the *Rounddown function*, if you want to round to the nearest given place. The *FLOOR function* is used to round down to the nearest specific multiple.

In Excel, it is possible to truncate decimal places using the *TRUNC function*. Moreover, you can round down and return an integer only using the *INT function*.

The Roundup function is applied to round up numbers to the nearest specified place.

You can round up to the nearest specified multiple using the *CEILING function*.

The Sort Function and How to Use it

If you want to use the *SORT function*, click on the range of cells you want to sort. Choose the data tab on the Ribbon. Then, tap on the *Sort command*. This will cause the sort dialog box to be displayed.

Choose either an ascending or descending sorting order for the cells. After sorting the cells satisfactorily, you should tap on the *OK icon*. With this, you can sort the cell range according to the chosen column.

But, if you want to sort data within the grid, use the *SORTBY function*. This is very flexible since you can apply deletion or addition features in the columns. The reason is that it refers to a range. However, the SORT function refers to a column index number.

It is useful in rearranging the records and fields in your data list or table of data.

The Sum Function and How to Use it

In a range of cells, the SUM Function is used for totaling one or more numbers. Click on a blank cell in the row under the cells you want to sum.

Then, scroll to the *Home menu* on the Ribbon and click on the *AutoSum button*. This will provide a SUM function in the highlighted cells automatically. It totals one or more numbers in a range of cells.

Another method is using the keyboard shortcut, which is ALT + =. Then, you will see a SUM formula in the active cell. Extend the frame of the cells to include cells that are not automatically added.

Tap on the *Enter button* to finish the setup.

Another way is entering functions manually in your worksheet. The syntax for SUM function setup is SUM (number1, [number 2],....).

The manual setup has a required argument, which is *number1*. Other optional arguments are enclosed in square brackets such as [number2],…

You can just type them inside the formula or they can exist as cell references.

The RoundUp Function and How to Use it

The RoundUp function returns a number rounded up to a specified number of the decimal places. Therefore, you can round up a number up to a specific number of digits. The return value is a rounded number.

The syntax for this function is =ROUNDUP (number, num_digits). In the arguments, the *number* means the number that you want to round up while num_digits stands for the digits you should round up the functions.

The RoundUp function is used to round numbers up. Negative numbers round to the left of the decimal while positive numbers round to the right of the decimal. Then, zero rounds to the nearest figure to it.

The RandBetween Function and How to Use it

This function is classified under Math and Trigonometry. It returns a random integer between user-specified numbers. Whenever the worksheet is opened or calculated, it will return a random integer.

Now, if you want to produce a range of random integers in several cells. Tap on the cells and enter the Randbetween function. Click on *Ctrl + Enter buttons.*

If you want to get a random number that may not be altered if the worksheet is calculated, go to the formula bar and enter *Randbetween.* Then, press F9 and convert the formula into the result.

To handle random numbers in Excel, highlight cell A1. Type RAND() and tap on the *Enter icon.* If you decide to generate a list of random numbers, highlight Cell A1. Tap on the lower right side of Cell A1 and drag it downwards.

Another strategy is copying the random numbers and pasting them as values. Then, select Cell C1 and view at the formula bar.

With this random function, you can produce random decimal numbers regarded as real numbers between 0 and 1.

The sign RAND() is a volatile function. It entails that whenever a worksheet is calculated a new random number is produced.

Math Functions in Excel 2021

In Excel, Math functions are arranged by entering the equal symbol before numeric values. These are numbers that you intend to calculate, including the Math operators you want to apply. This pattern is strictly for simple formulas.

There is the plus sign (+) for addition and the minus sign (-) for subtraction. The slash (/) is for division while the asterisk (*) is for multiplication.

Some of the Math functions in Excel include the SUM () function, the SUMIF () function, the COUNT () function, the SYNTAX () function, the AVERAGE () function, etc.

The RoundDown Function and How to Use it

The Rounddown function is designed to round a number to zero. The syntax is Rounddown(number, num_digits).

This syntax comes with arguments such as *number,* which is required and it is any real number that you want to round down. The num_digits, which is required is the number of digits that you want to round the number.

When the num_digts are greater than zero, then the number is rounded down to the given number of decimal places. But if num_digits is zero, the number is rounded down to the nearest integer. However, if the num_digits is less than zero, the number is rounded down to the left side of the decimal place.

The SUMIF Function and How to Use it

This function is used for returning the number of cells that satisfy a given condition. It can be applied to numbers, dates, and even texts.

The SUMIF function returns incorrect outcomes if you apply it for matching strings longer than the string value or 255 characters.

The syntax for SUMIF is =SUMIF(range, criteria, [sum_range]).

The argument is that the range is necessary, which should be assessed by the criteria. Every range should have numbers containing arrays, numbers, names, and references.

The criteria are necessary and appear in the form of text, cell reference, function, and number. You may add wildcard figures such as question marks (?), asterisks (*), etc.

The sum_range is optional and represents the real cells to add.

Handling a SUMIF Function with Multiple Criteria

This SUMIF function is applied to sum cells that met several criteria. SUMIFs are used for summing cells that are adjacent and meet criteria such as numbers, texts, and dates.

Logical operators are supported by SUMIF functions. These operators include:

- = - equals to
- < - less than
- > - greater than
- <> - not equal to

The syntax for SUMIF is =SUMIF(sum_range, range1, criteria1, [range2], [criteria2], …

From the syntax above, the sum_range is the range to be summed. Range 1 is the first range to be evaluated. Criteria1 is the criteria to use on range 1. Range 2 is optional for analysis while criteria 2 is optional to be used on range 2.

SUMIFS involves eight functions that divide logical criteria into two parts, which are range and criteria. Therefore, the syntax for developing criteria is different while SUMIF uses a range of cells for range arguments. It is not possible to use an array.

Chapter 16

EXCEL CALENDAR WITH JUST ONE FORMULA

Creating a Calendar (Calendar Format)

1. Use a new blank worksheet or a new workbook
2. Input the start date in cell B3
3. Input the weekdays starting on Sunday in B6

◢ A	B	C	D	E	F	G	H
1							
2							
3	2/1/2020						
4							
5							
6	Sunday	Monday	Tuesday	Wednesday	Thursday	Friday	Saturday
7							
8							

4. In B7, input this formula:

- =SEQUENCE(5,7, IF(WEEKDAY(B3,2)=7,B3,B3-WEEKDAY(B3,2)),1)

You'll get this:

A	B	C	D	E	F	G	H
1							
2							
3	2/1/2020						
4							
5							
6	Sunday	Monday	Tuesday	Wednesday	Thursday	Friday	Saturday
7	43856	43857	43858	43859	43860	43861	43862
8	43863	43864	43865	43866	43867	43868	43869
9	43870	43871	43872	43873	43874	43875	43876
10	43877	43878	43879	43880	43881	43882	43883
11	43884	43885	43886	43887	43888	43889	43890
12							

5. Format the results to a date format

A	B	C	D	E	F	G	H
1							
2							
3	2/1/2020						
4							
5							
6	Sunday	Monday	Tuesday	Wednesday	Thursday	Friday	Saturday
7	1/26/2020	1/27/2020	1/28/2020	1/29/2020	1/30/2020	1/31/2020	2/1/2020
8	2/2/2020	2/3/2020	2/4/2020	2/5/2020	2/6/2020	2/7/2020	2/8/2020
9	2/9/2020	2/10/2020	2/11/2020	2/12/2020	2/13/2020	2/14/2020	2/15/2020
10	2/16/2020	2/17/2020	2/18/2020	2/19/2020	2/20/2020	2/21/2020	2/22/2020
11	2/23/2020	2/24/2020	2/25/2020	2/26/2020	2/27/2020	2/28/2020	2/29/2020
12							

Technically speaking, the calendar is finished. The issue is that SEQUENCE will always start on the first Sunday of every month, even if that day is not part of the month of interest. The solution is to use conditional formatting to hide days that are not part of the month specified in B3.

6. Highlight the entire month result set (B7:H11)
7. In the Home tab, click on Conditional Formatting
8. Click on New Rule
9. Click on 'Use a formula to determine which cells to format'
10. Use this formula:
=Month(B3)<>Month(B7)

Note that B4 is absolute (with the $ signs) and B7 is relative (without the $ signs)

This formula will return TRUE or FALSE if the month in B3 is not part of the month of the monthly cells.

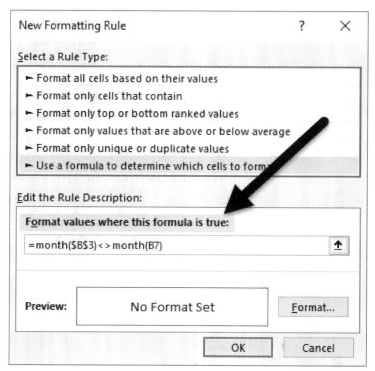

Conditional formatting rules will only apply to cells where the condition is TRUE. *If the month is not in January, then it will be TRUE,* and we can hide it.

11. Click on Format
12. An easy way to hide numbers is to make the font the same color as the background, in this case, white

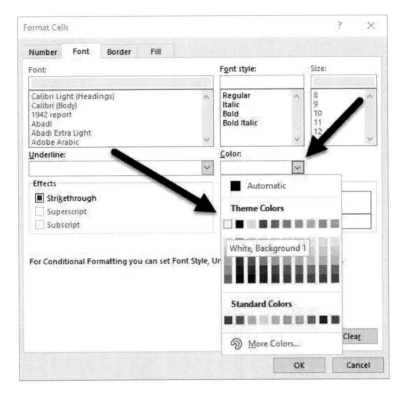

13. Click OK
14. Click OK

There's your calendar built with 1 formula and 1 conditional format.

	A	B	C	D	E	F	G	H
1								
2								
3		1/1/2020						
4								
5								
6		Sunday	Monday	Tuesday	Wednesday	Thursday	Friday	Saturday
7					1/1/2020	1/2/2020	1/3/2020	1/4/2020
8		1/5/2020	1/6/2020	1/7/2020	1/8/2020	1/9/2020	1/10/2020	1/11/2020
9		1/12/2020	1/13/2020	1/14/2020	1/15/2020	1/16/2020	1/17/2020	1/18/2020
10		1/19/2020	1/20/2020	1/21/2020	1/22/2020	1/23/2020	1/24/2020	1/25/2020
11		1/26/2020	1/27/2020	1/28/2020	1/29/2020	1/30/2020	1/31/2020	
12								

How to Make a Schedule in Excel

Here, I will be teaching you how to create a weekly schedule. Provided you are able to create the weekly schedule, all other schedules will not be difficult to create.

Creating a Weekly Schedule

To create a weekly schedule, follow the procedure below:

From the **View** tab, click on the **Page layout** to switch the worksheet view

In the Page **Layout tab**, Click on **Margin** and select **Wide**

Move to cells **A3 and A4** to input the time (**8:00 AM and 8:30 AM** respectively) and then use the drag handle to autofill the time to **6:00 PM**

Move to cells B1 and C1 to input the date (**3/25/2019 and 3/26/2019** respectively) and use the drag handle to autofill the date to **3/31/2019**

Move to cell **B2** to input the days of the week starting with **Monday** and then drag with the autofill handle to **Sunday**

Select the list of data on the worksheet except for the **date**

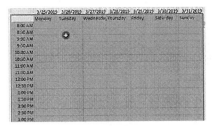

To add a table, go to the **Home tab**, click on the **Format Table** and select any table of your choice

Select **My table has header** and click on **Ok**

Here, the worksheet is formatted with the table

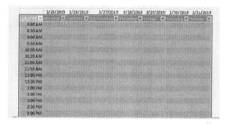

To change the color of the cells that contain the date, highlight the cells and select the **Format tool**

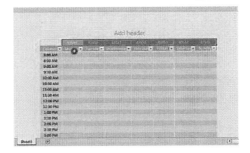

You change the **column** heading to **time** by clicking on the cell that contains column

Chapter 17

ULTIMATE EXCEL TIPS AND TRICKS FOR 2022

Renaming a Sheet with a Double Click

There are various ways to rename sheets in Excel and the easiest of them all is by double-clicking on the sheet and then renaming it.

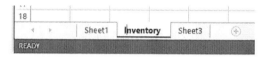

Changing the Case of a Text

Certain functions are used to change the case of a text. For Example, the UPPER function capitalizes all the characters, the LOWER function changes the text to lower case while the PROPER function capitalizes the first character of a text.

C8		f_x	=UPPER(A8)			
	A	B	C	D	E	F	G
1	JOHN						
2	GRACE	13					
3	LOVE	33					
4							
5	JOY	22					
6	ADAMS	33					
7							
8	ayo	22	AYO				

149

Forming a Text with &

With the sign & you can join the texts in different columns into a single cell. Let's join cells A2, B2, C2, and D4 to form JOYUSA23F in cell F2.

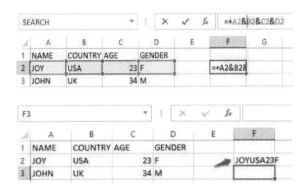

How to Make Excel Show Leading Zero

When a value starts with zero, Excel will automatically delete the zero. To avoid this problem, add a single quote mark before the zero as shown in the table below.

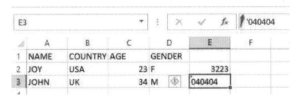

Extending Formula Down

You can extend the formula from a cell by dragging the + cross at the lower bottom corner of the cell and moving to the other cells.

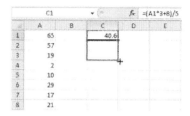

Changing How Enter Works

When you click on **Enter** by default, it moves you down to a cell. You can change the method of how Enter works in another direction. To do this;

Go to **File** and move to **Options**

Click on the **Advanced** tab and go to **Edit Options**

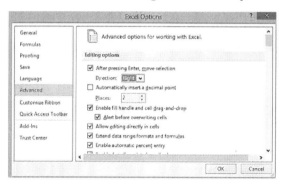

Quick Select Formulas

This feature can help save time when trying to input formulas into the cells. As you begin to type the formula, you can scroll down to choose out of the suggested formulas and use the Enter to select the formula automatically.

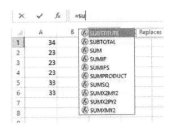

Disabling the Excel Start Screen

Probably you hate it when you open your Excel program only to be welcomed with Excel Start Screen. To disable the Start Screen;

Go to **File** and move to **Options**

Go to **General** and move **to Start-up options** to disable the Excel Start Screen

Then click on **Ok**

Activating Current Date and Time

You can insert the current date and time by using the NOW function by using the date and time from the system.

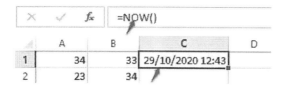

The Status Bar

When you right-click on the status bar, there are a lot of features available you can add.

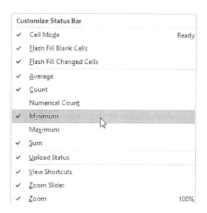

Deleting Errors Cells

To get rid of cells with error values;

From the **Home tab,** go to **Editing** and click on **Find & Replace**

Go to **Go To Special** and in the **Go To Special** dialog box, select **Formula** and then tick **Errors**

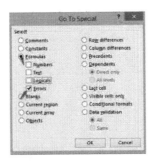

Striking Through Texts in Excel

To strike through texts in Excel, all you need to do is first select the cell and then press **Ctrl + 5**

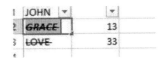

How to Clear Formatting

You can clear any formatting from a cell or a range of cells. To do this;

From the **Home tab,** go to **Editing**

Select **Clear** and click on **Clear Format**

Sharing Data Online on Excel

You can share Excel data or documents online. By implication, you can collaborate with another person to work along with you on the Excel worksheet. Not only that, you don't have to go around with your computer, you can choose to save your data to OneCloud and make reference to it anytime, anywhere.

To share Excel files online;

From the File menu back view, go to **Share**.

Then choose any of the options that pop up (***Invite People, Email, and Save to OneDrive***).

NOTE: To save your data or files on ***OneCloud***, you must have Microsoft Account on your computer.

Free Add-Ins for Excel to Start Using Now

- ASAP utilities developed by Andrew Engwirda
- Autosafe developed by Jan Karel
- Findlink developed by Bill Manville
- Menurighter developed by Doug Glancy
- Name manager developed by Jan Karel
- Xlg favorites developed by Ken Puls

CONCLUSION

Thank you for reading this book. Excel skills are some of those skills that have become very important in the job market today. They carry a lot of weight because Excel does not just represent one type of skill, but a wide range of skills that employers are interested in so much. That is why people with good Excel skills stand a better chance of securing a job than those people who have little or no knowledge about the spreadsheet.

Once you have mastered the material in this book, you are ready for all the other things that can be done with Excel.

Now that you have read this book, you can handle all tasks and projects on your Excel worksheet. No matter the sector where you work, in corporate organizations, financial institutions, agricultural sectors, or a private business enterprise, it is a veritable tool, which you can apply to handle your records properly.

Overall, Microsoft Excel assists you in manipulating, monitoring, and interpreting data, allowing you to make better choices and save time and money.

Excel is used for accountants, investment managers, consultants, and individuals in all aspects of financial careers to fulfill their everyday tasks. With the internet playing such an important role in our lives and businesses, it's only natural that the interests of many would win out. Staying up to date on new technology has been a full-time task as Microsoft platforms continue to grow. Microsoft Excel will continue to be the most popular framework for analyzing results, creating maps and presentations, and integrating with powerful software for digital dashboards and business intelligence workflows.

Excel is often unavoidable in marketing, but with the tips mentioned above, it doesn't have to be so intimidating. Practice makes perfect, as they say. These formulae, shortcuts, and methods will become second nature the more you utilize them.

Excel skills will make things much easier for you in a job setting. For instance, you can gather data easily if you are required to, analyze it if this is needed, and also draw some conclusions from the data. Sometimes you might be required to present a section of that data to people who make decisions for the business. You need excellent Excel skills to be able to do this and this is what will help you advance in your career from one rank to the other.

Getting a job today is not as easy as it was some years ago. People are studying really hard in order to get skills that will land them good jobs. You only need the right skills and you will have the job of your dreams. Many employers do not consider how many skills you have but what you can actually do with the skills that you have, even if you have just a few skills. This is what generates results in the end and it is what matters to the right people.

Good luck!!!

Made in the USA
Coppell, TX
08 March 2022

74653970R00087